The Conquest of Mexico

Miguel Gómez

ANDREA PRESS

Author: Miguel Gómez

Illustrator: Jose Ignacio Redondo

Editorial Director: Javier Huerta

Published by:
ANDREA PRESS
C/ Talleres, 21
Pol. Ind. de Alpedrete
28430 Alpedrete (Madrid)
Tel: 91 857 00 08
Fax: 91 857 00 48
www.andrea-miniatures.com
andrea@andrea-miniatures.com

Origin of images:
Album - 16, 32, 37, 63, 64, 77, 94
Private collection - 45a, 45b
Corbis - 4, 8, 12, 13, 18, 22, 24, 25, 33, 60, 65,
72, 80, 85, 90a, 90b, 98, 111b
Oronoz - 14, 43, 44, 45c, 46, 47, 49a, 49b, 52,
53, 54, 55, 59, 71, 73, 76, 79, 81, 83, 88, 91,
101, 104, 105, 108, 110, 111a

Computer graphics and maps:
Javier Huerta

Layout:
ANDREA PRESS

Printed in Spain
by ATIG

Inside Cover
Details of a page from the Tudela Codex,
created by the Aztecs, annoted in Castillian.
Museum of Madrid

ISBN.: 978-84-96658-05-9

INDEX

PROLOGUE

Spanish history includes several episodes that are incomprehensible to modern thought. Episodes where the enterprise itself was of less importance than the pursuit of valour, through the taking of huge risks to the point of rashness, utmost boldness and the will to progress, all in the name of the Christian Faith and Empire. One of these episodes is the conquest of Mexico, in which a handful of men, led by Hernán Cortés, undertook a heroic adventure, the story of which has been handed down through the generations. Naturally, as with any historical episode, the overview must include background information, the circumstances under which the particular episode took place and the characteristics of the protagonists, including all the different facets of their characters, and the progression of well-known events. This is exactly the way in which this episode, ignored by some, condemned by others, is treated in Miguel Gómez's book, which overcomes modern prejudices that tend to tarnish historical objectivity.

The author, who is, without doubt, a pre-eminent world historian, uncovers the time when the conquest took place. He writes initially about the Mesoamerican civilizations, with emphasis on the Mexica Empire, composed of a warlike, highly organized and fearsome people; after that, he examines the Spanish Crown and the Spanish temperament, also made up of religious and belligerent people, with internal conflicts that eventually achieved the re-conquering and the unification of the Iberian peninsula in the name of Christ while, simultaneously, conquering the New World. Furthermore, Miguel Gómez describes in much detail the characteristics of both civilizations, highlighting their military organisations, to give the reader a clear idea of the conditions under which the conquest took place.

Although the tone of the book is objective, it is not exempt from adjectives that are consistent throughout. The information is expressed with clarity and supported by magnificent illustrations so that the reader becomes immersed in a narrative as passionate as the events themselves. We will accompany Cortés on his journey to Tenochtitlán, the impressive city in the heart of Mexicas, where he will face numerous enemies but also have the support of some natives, to confront the powerful Moctezuma. Gómez does not overlook the dark episodes that took place, primarily due to the personalities and nature of the dominant characters.

The continuation of the history lives on in this new work, through the fusion of Miguel Gómez's text, Jose Ignacio Redondo's illustrations and Javier Huerta's graphic assistance. It is a splendid book that, without doubt, will assist the reader in learning and understanding one of the greatest heroic deeds that changed the course of the world.

Fermín de los Reyes Gómez
Professor of Bibliography
Complutense University of Madrid

◀

HERNÁN CORTÉS AND MOCTEZUMA

A romantic rendering showing Hernán Cortés, in complete armour, and Moctezuma II in a finely decorated cape and shield

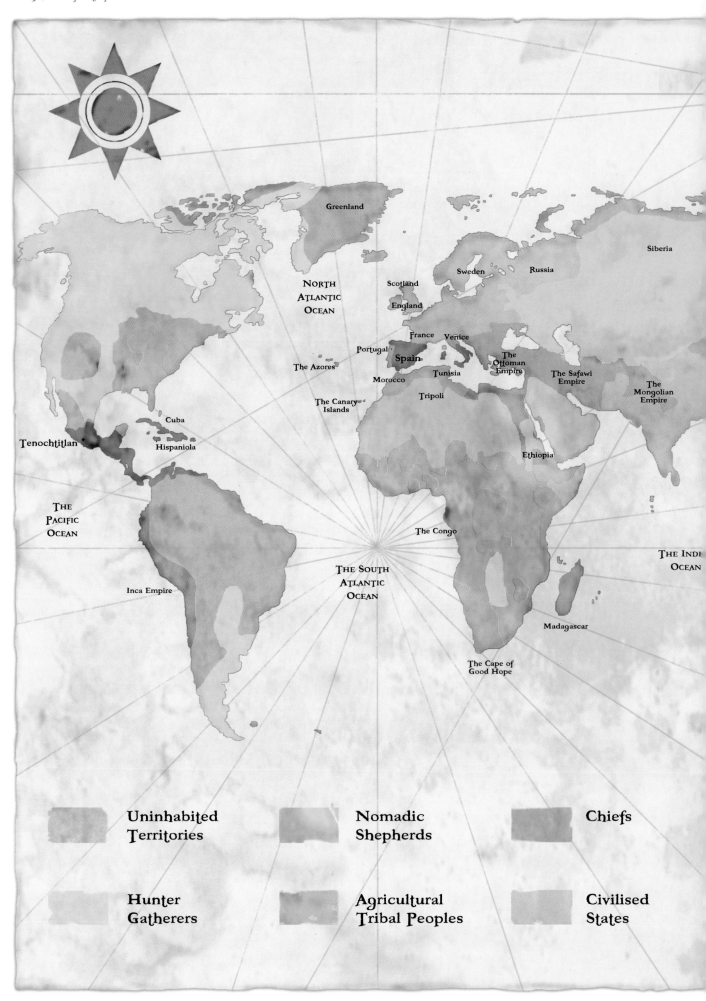

Greenland

Siberia

NORTH
ATLANTIC
OCEAN

Scotland

England

Sweden

Russia

France   Venice

Portugal

Spain

The
Ottoman
Empire

The Safawi
Empire

The
Mongolian
Empire

The Azores

Morocco

Tunisia

Cuba

Tripoli

The Canary
Islands

Tenochtitlan

Hispaniola

Ethiopia

THE
PACIFIC
OCEAN

The Congo

THE IND[
OCEAN

THE SOUTH
ATLANTIC
OCEAN

Inca Empire

Madagascar

The Cape of
Good Hope

	Uninhabited Territories		Nomadic Shepherds		Chiefs
	Hunter Gatherers		Agricultural Tribal Peoples		Civilised States

THE WORLD IN THE 16TH CENTURY

The Chinese Empire

The Spanish Empire

Other Empires

The 16th Century marks one of the main points of inflection in the history of humanity. Many of the changes that began during the 15th Century finally materialized in the 16th Century giving way to the appearance of still more flagrant ruptures in the course of the events. The European Middle Ages was finally totally buried and, with it, much of the religious and superstitious visions that existed during that time, while the humanism of the Renaissance took its first tentative steps. Universal knowledge emanated from the monasteries and, thanks to Gutenberg and his press, the cornerstone of the popularisation of culture had begun. The changes were deep. The discovery of the New World opened here-to-fore unknown horizons for the Europeans. Centralised states began to consolidate under absolute monarchies. The feudal panorama of small and large manors, with the power in the hands of the rural nobility, yielded before powerful sovereigns who governed with a firm hand. The new order, supported by ministers of courtly nobility, meant the great majority had to leave their property to transfer the capital to the Court.

Philip II, the monarch of the Spanish Empire, is a paradigmatic example of this. In contrast to him, his father, Emperor Charles, was a restless traveller, while Philip governed his empire from his capital, Madrid, surrounding himself with able civil servants. Philip was a bureaucratic king who favoured centralisation and the strengthening of the crown to the detriment of the nobility. With this governmental policy, the cities continued to gain specific power in European society and with them their ruling classes, the mercantile bourgeoisie and craftsmen, who in later centuries would cease to hold the reins of power, especially at the start of the French Revolution.

Military tactics quickly changed thanks to the emergence of firearms. The disciplined squadrons of infantry, armed with pikes and crossbows, defeated the here-to-fore unbeatable medieval cavalry. The Catholic Church could not escape these changes and saw a considerable decrease in its power and influence in spite of its efforts to reform the face of its organisation. Stained and discredited by medieval vices: corruption, ignorance and sexual promiscuity, the Catholic Church had to

◀ *THE 16TH CENTURY*

In the 16th Century, empires and highly developed civilisations coexisted with primitive cultures and vast unpopulated and unknown territories.

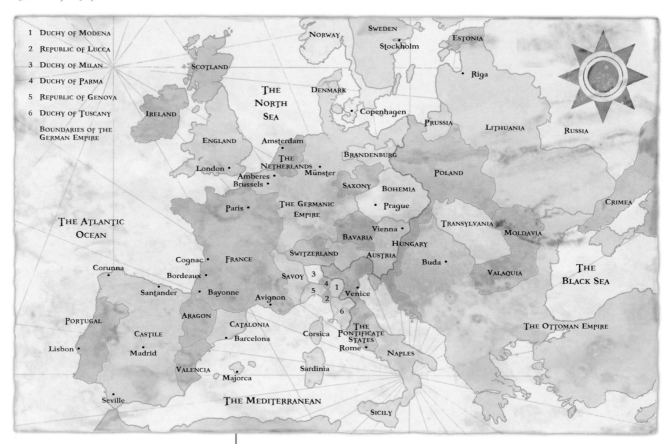

1 DUCHY OF MODENA
2 REPUBLIC OF LUCCA
3 DUCHY OF MILAN
4 DUCHY OF PARMA
5 REPUBLIC OF GENOVA
6 DUCHY OF TUSCANY
BOUNDARIES OF THE
GERMAN EMPIRE

NORWAY
SWEDEN
Stockholm
ESTONIA
Riga
SCOTLAND
DENMARK
Copenhagen
PRUSSIA
LITHUANIA
RUSSIA
THE NORTH SEA
IRELAND
ENGLAND
Amsterdam
BRANDENBURG
THE NETHERLANDS
Münster
POLAND
London
Amberes
Brussels
SAXONY
BOHEMIA
CRIMEA
Paris
THE GERMANIC EMPIRE
Prague
THE ATLANTIC OCEAN
Vienna
TRANSYLVANIA
BAVARIA
MOLDAVIA
Cognac
FRANCE
SWITZERLAND
AUSTRIA
HUNGARY
Corunna
Bordeaux
SAVOY
3
Buda
VALAQUIA
THE BLACK SEA
Santander
Bayonne
4
1
5
Venice
Avignon
2
PORTUGAL
ARAGON
6
THE PONTIFICATE STATES
THE OTTOMAN EMPIRE
CASTILE
CATALONIA
Corsica
Rome
Lisbon
Barcelona
Naples
Madrid
VALENCIA
Sardinia
Seville
Majorca
SICILY
THE MEDITERRANEAN

▲

EUROPE IN THE MIDDLE OF THE 16TH CENTURY
The Austrian Hapsburg dynasty dominated Europe and governed the Kingdom of Spain as well as its incipient colonial territories and the Holy Roman Empire.

face up to the Lutheran Reformation. Martin Luther received unconditional support from the German princes and the Nordic states and saw a golden opportunity in the lessons of the German monks to shake Papal repression centred on Rome. Consequently, Protestantism was able to extend quickly to northern Europe, in spite of the military efforts of Emperor Charles to contain it.

Adding yet more tension to the situation was the Turkish Empire, and its conquest of Constantinople in 1453, which continually threatened Eastern Europe.

The rest of the world did not remain unaffected by this. Islam extended from North Africa to Central Asia and it moved around the Ottoman Empire and the Safavid, centralised in old Persia. Ivan the Terrible laid the foundations of the future Russian Empire. Also, in spite of the navigations and discoveries of the Portuguese explorers, Africa continued to be relatively unknown and the Mongol dynasty, inherited from Tamerlane and Genghis Khan, grew stronger in India.

On the Indian subcontinent, monotheist Islam and polytheist Hinduism gave rise to years of tolerance and the enrichment of understanding, with Emperor Akbar as the principal figure; Muslim by faith, eclectic in his government. The Ming Empire in China began to weaken and, despite The Great Wall, it could not avoid collapse and fell into the hands of the Manchurians.

At the beginning of the century, Japan was divided into almost four hundred independent states commanded by warlords of the armed forces that continuously fought against one another. This devastating panorama finally ended with the restoration of the Shogunate of the Tokugawa that ensured almost two hundred years of peace in the country.

The five great religions of the world: Hinduism, Buddhism, Judaism, Christianity and Islam had already extended to Asia, Europe and most of

THE EARTH AS CENTRE OF THE UNIVERSE

Despite the scientific advances made during the Renaissance, civilised society continued to believe that the Earth was the centre of the Universe and the rest of the cosmos revolved around it.

▶

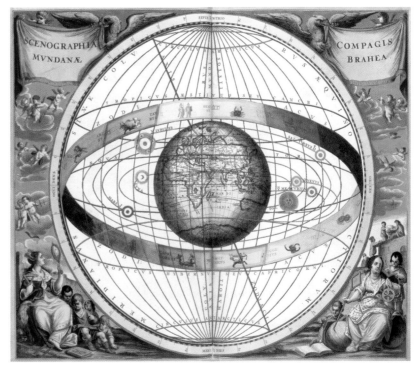

THE GREAT EXPLORERS

The great navigators of the 16th Century were Portuguese and Spanish. Thanks to their explorations, Europe began to discover the world.

▼

North Africa. Australia, Oceania and a large part of the Americas, yet to be discovered, remained uncivilised.

The Incas, who had been able to fortify and consolidate an Andean empire by conquering and absorbing the cultures that existed there, reigned across South America. Despite this, they could not escape the human internal divisions and the *Tahuantinsuyu* was torn by a civil war between the princes and brothers, Atahualpa and Huascar. This civil war set the scene for the destruction of the empire at the hands of Pizarro and his men. The other centre of civilization in the Americas was in Central America. From 1800 B.C., the cultures and cities flourished with city-states taking over, disappearing and then re-emerging. At the beginning of 16th Century, the Aztec Empire governed the Mexican plateau from the valley of the Anahuac. As the heirs to refined cultures, it was a young, dynamic and expanding empire with a promising future whose tragic end could not be foreseen.

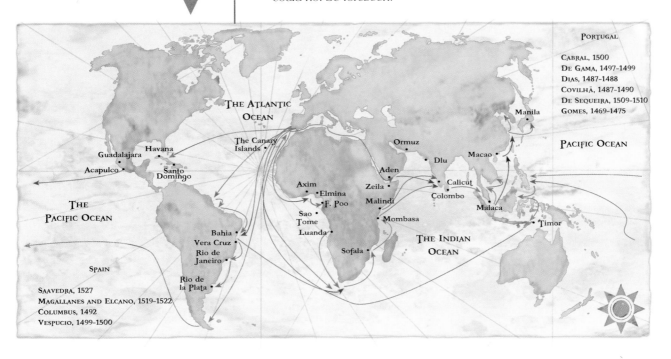

PORTUGAL

CABRAL, 1500
DE GAMA, 1497-1499
DIAS, 1487-1488
COVILHÃ, 1487-1490
DE SEQUEIRA, 1509-1510
GOMES, 1469-1475

PACIFIC OCEAN

THE ATLANTIC OCEAN

Manila

The Canary Islands

Guadalajara · Havana

Acapulco · Santo Domingo

Ormuz

Macao

Dlu

Aden

Axim

Zeila · Calicut

Elmina

F. Poo · Malindi · Colombo

Sao Tome

Malaca

Luanda · Mombasa

Timor

THE PACIFIC OCEAN

Bahia

Vera Cruz

Rio de Janeiro

Sofala

THE INDIAN OCEAN

Rio de la Plata

SPAIN

SAAVEDRA, 1527
MAGALLANES AND ELCANO, 1519-1522
COLUMBUS, 1492
VESPUCIO, 1499-1500

MEXICO THE FIRST SETTLERS

I t is impossible to determine the exact moment in history when man first crossed the Bering Straits. The Paleo-Indian culture of Clovis in present day New Mexico appeared thirteen or fourteen thousand years ago, and is considered the culture from which all other American Indian cultures descended. However, Paleo-Indian archaeological remains have been found as old as the one of Clovis, in Monteverde in southern Chile. There remains much controversy and continued investigation into how long it took the first Americans to migrate the ten thousand miles from the Bering Straits to southern Chile.

THE MESOAMERICAN CIVILIZATIONS

The development of agriculture is the foundation upon which the civilizations were built. In Central America, or Mesoamerica, they not only discovered agriculture but they also invented the cultivation of corn, a plant that did not exist in the wild and was developed by the Indians.

Where corn flourished, so did advanced cultures. Four centres of regional power existed around organised state cities in Mesoamerica. These was the Central River basin in the North, where the city of Teotihuacan emerged and, later, where the Toltecs settled. In the region of Oaxaca, there were powerful and prosperous chieftainships. The Olmecs established themselves along the coast of the Gulf of Mexico and, finally, the Mayans in Guatemala and the Yucatan peninsula.

The first Mesoamerican civilization was the Olmecs (1800 B.C.-200 B.C.). The theocratic structure of its society drove the construction of the first pyramidal structured temples. In the middle of the tropical forests of the Gulf of Mexico, they developed monumental artistic expressions, such as the famous heads, and refined ceramics. Both the mysteries of its religious cult and other cultural manifestations served as the inspiration and origin for the other Mesoamerican civilizations. Privileged students of the Olmecs were the Zapotecs, who, by around the year 600 B.C. already had their own capital, Monte Albán, in the region of Oaxaca. The Zapotecs developed fundamental

◀ *CORNFIELDS*
The origin of the Mesoamerican civilisation is found in the development and perfection of the planting of corn.

11

OLMEC MONUMENTAL
SCULPTURE
These heads are the first examples
of a civilised culture in all of
America.

THE FIRST MESOAMERICAN
CULTURES
The first known inhabitants of
Mesoamerica were the states of
Teotihuacan (200 A.D. - 900 A.D.),
Zapotecs (600 B.C. - 800 A.D.),
Olmecs (1800 B.C. - 200 B.C.) and
the Mayans (250 A.D. - 950 A.D.)

elements of the Mexican cultures such as writing, mathematics and the calendar. They also attained a very high level of astronomical observation that was later perfected by the Mayans.

In the central region of Mexico two important cities appeared, Cuicuilco and Teotihuacan. After the destruction of the former by a volcanic eruption, Teotihuacan became the predominant city of the region. Its monumental architecture with its enormous pyramids was developed at the start of 250 A.D. Tlaloc, the God of Rain, and the famous Quetzalcoatl, the Lead Serpent, were their principal deities both of which played a notable role in the events of later centuries. The city was abandoned in 900 A.D. and by the time the Spaniards arrived only majestic ruins remained.

Between the 250 A.D. and 1150 A.D., another important civilization on the Gulf coast emerged. This was around the region of Veracruz and became known as the Tajín civilization, probably of Totonaca origin. In addition to its monumental and religious architecture, the Tajín civilization was also known for its significant number of *Tlachtli* courts, a ball game founded in their cities. *Tlachtli* was a pre-Columbian ball game popular with the Mesoamerican cultures. As with most aspects of those civilizations, it was full of religious connotations. It is said that the Aztecs, who were great fans of the game, would sacrifice the losing team before their thirsty Gods. Perhaps, the most remarkable civilization of pre-Columbian Mexico, were the Mayans, who reached a level of impressive cultural development thanks to advances made by Olmecs, Zapotecs and certainly the Teotihuacan civilizations.

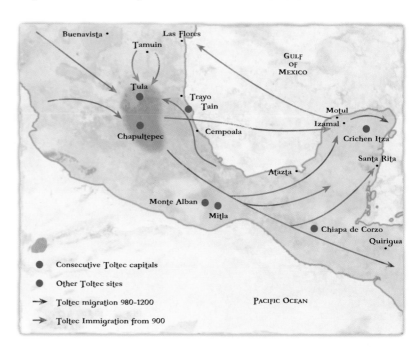

● Consecutive Toltec capitals
● Other Toltec sites
→ Toltec migration 980-1200
→ Toltec Immigration from 900

▲

The Pyramid of the Sun in Teotihuacan.
By the time the Spaniards arrived, the city was no more than majestic ruins.

◄

Migrations of the Toltecs
A barbarian tribe, or Chichimec, that attained an impressive cultural development in the Valley of Mexico and the Yucatan peninsula. The Aztecs declared themselves their heirs.

The Toltecs

The Toltecs first appeared on the Mexican scene around 950 A.D. originating from the north and guided by the chieftain leader, *Mixcoatl Ce Tecpatl*, 'One Sacrificial Knife'. After conquering several towns and cities, they decided to establish their capital on the plains of central Mexico. Thus was born Tollan, later known as Tula.

They declared themselves followers of Quetzalcoatl, the main deity of their pantheon, and acquired the name of Toltecs, meaning 'Excellent Artist' in the *Nahuatl* language.

Quetzalcoatl is a mythical figure whose influence extended throughout Mexico, from the North to the Mayan cultures where it went under the name of *Kukulkán*. This deity distanced itself from human sacrifices and advocated a more tolerant religious sense.

'The Lead Serpent created man with its own blood and gave him corn to feed himself. I taught man how to polish jade, I gave man the calendar and he set the days of prayers and sacrifices.'

Inspired by Quetzalcoatl, the Toltecs unified the power of the Mesoamerican civilizations. They inherited the culture and the dominion of Teotihuacan and, at the height of its splendour its influence extended throughout western Mexico, including the Yucatan peninsula. The Toltecs left an indelible mark on the Mexican identity, which remained in the centuries following the conquest; their culture and achievements made them the most legendary people of all Mesoamerica. However, by the time of the arrival of the Aztecs, Toltec power had dissipated through internal fighting between ancestors and rival cities.

THE AZTECS

Around 1000 A.D., Mexico underwent fundamental changes. The great cultures of the Mexican Classic period were weakening, in some cases going as far as the abandonment of their cities, as happened in Teotihuacan in the centre of the Mayan civilisation in the south. New tribes of nomads and harvesters, called Chichimecs (equivalent to barbarian or savage), migrated from the north and appeared on the Mesoamerican scene. The sedentary, corn-cultivating towns with great cultural development were invaded by the barbarians from the North, migrating from the south of present day United States, following a similar process to that of the fall of the Roman Empire in Europe. However, unlike the Germanic tribes, the Chichimecs absorbed the conquered cultures making them their own and taking them to a new or greater level. The Toltecs are a clear example of this.

This process of immigration occurred during centuries parallel with the development of the new city state.

Several of these migrations that composed Chichimecs towns are said to originate from *Aztlan*, an indeterminate place in northern Mexico that scholars have been unable to locate. The term Aztec derives from Aztlán (Aztec word for 'the white island'). Notwithstanding, Aztecs never referred to themselves that way, but as Mexicas (village) or Tenochcas, followers of Tenoch, and the leader who led them during their migration. According to their own legend, it was their Huitzilopochtli deity, through the word of his Cuauhtloquezqui priest that persuaded them to leave their place of origin in search of a glorious destiny that would allow them to reign in the other villages. The search for glory was not an exclusive European trait. Tenoch's pilgrimage had to continue until he found a sign from his God: *'That is where our home will be, Mexico-Tenochtitlan, the place where the eagle cries, spreads its wings and eats, the place where fish swim, the place where the serpent is torn. In Mexico-Tenochtitlan, many things will happen.'*

AMBITIOUS MERCENARIES

Nahuatl was the language of the Mexicas as well as the Toltecs. Unlike the Toltecs, who had by then developed a refined culture, the Mexicas had nothing. They were true savages, harvesters and hunters.

◀ *TENOCHTITLAN*
The Aztec capital.
Works exhibited in the National History Mural Museum (Mexico DF)

EXPANSION OF THE AZTEC EMPIRE

In little less than two centuries, the Mexicas went from being a pariah tribe on the Mexican plateau to sovereigns of a great empire.

▶

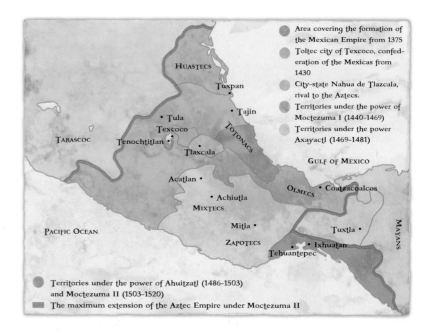

- Area covering the formation of the Mexican Empire from 1375
- Toltec city of Texcoco, confederation of the Mexicas from 1430
- City-state Nahua de Tlazcala, rival to the Aztecs.
- Territories under the power of Moctezuma I (1440-1469)
- Territories under the power Axayactl (1469-1481)

HUASTECS
Tuxpan
Tajin
Tula
Texcoco
TOTONACS
TARASCOC
Tenochtitlan
Tlaxcala
GULF OF MEXICO
Acatlan
OLMECS • Coatzacoalcos
Achiutla
MIXTECS
PACIFIC OCEAN
Mitla
Tuxtla
MAYANS
ZAPOTECS • Ixhuatan
Tehuantepec

- Territories under the power of Ahuitzatl (1486-1503) and Moctezuma II (1503-1520)
- The maximum extension of the Aztec Empire under Moctezuma II

MEXICA CODEX

The Aztecs had a hieroglyphic script, allowing them to paint codices, or ancient manuscript texts. Just a few of these escaped the destruction of the Spanish friars.

▼

They are seen as a small tribe (around a thousand people) guided by a bloodthirsty god that promised them glory, wandering aimlessly in a valley where other cultures flourished and the cornfields that fed the cities were abundant and the towns prosperous. Their cruel character, emanating from being forced to base themselves in provisional areas like the Chapultepec forest and to conduct themselves as mercenaries, an activity that suited them well, meant that they were universally shunned. However, the tribe was ambitious; its God had promised them shining glory. Not content with their status as mercenaries under the power of others, the Mexicas conspired to improve their position by means of a political marriage. This practice was very common everywhere in the world, particularly between the European monarchies. Therefore, they asked the Chief of Culhuacan, of Toltec lineage, whose name was Achitometl, for the hand of his daughter for their God, Huitzilipochtli. The father could not foresee the tragic end for his daughter. Fulfilling their word, the Mexicas offered the young girl to their God. They sacrificed her on his altar and, once skinned, the priest, to impress the Divine, wore the maiden's skin. To escape the wrath of Achitometl, the tribe were forced to flee and place themselves under the protection of the Chief of Azcapotzalco. Their new masters, to whom they had to pay homage and tribute, gave them a home on a desert island in the middle of Lake Texcoco. It was an inhospitable place that seemed more an exile than a home but, around 1325, the Mexicas found their promised land because, upon a prickly pear they saw an eagle with a serpent in its beak. It was the sign prophesied by Huitzilipochtli.

THE EAGLE DEVOURING
A SERPENT, PERCHED
ON A CACTUS

*This was the prophesy indicating
the place from where the Mexica
capital of Tenochtitlan had to rise
and the end of the pilgrimage.*

▼

THE FOUNDATION OF TENOCHTITLAN

The Azcatitlan manuscript shows these first Mexicas in canoes, fishing with rods or nets surrounded by rushes and aquatic birds. Their neighbours knew them as *Atlaca Chichimeca*, the lacustrine savages. In all, they were pretty poverty stricken. When they needed wood and stones to build Huitzlipochtli's first sanctuary, (the first steps to the future Tenochtitlan) they had to go and get them from the urban tribes living on the banks of the lake in exchange for fish, aquatic birds and animals. Little-by-little, they increased their small settlement through an ingenious system of man-made islands. These were a type of enormous oval-shaped wicker baskets, anchored to the bottom of the shallow lake and filled with earth to act as receptacles suitable for sowing. Thus, Mexico-Tenochtitlan was being born through forced manual labour.

The small barren island, inhabited by a primitive people, went through a process of change influenced by the surrounding cultures with a strong Toltec inheritance. Around 1427 A.D., Tenochtitlan had become a consolidated city that viewed their neighbours on equal terms. The *Tlatoani* (sovereign) Itzacoatl, supported or rather inspired by its 'prime minister, *cihuacoatl* Tlacaelel, decided to shake off the repression inflicted by the ecpaneca Lords of Azcapotzalco. To do so, he proposed an alliance with the other lakeside cities. This was the origin of the Triple Alliance, which took control of the region and marked the beginning of what continues to be known as the Aztec Empire. The Triple Alliance was composed of the cities of Tenochtitlan, Texcoco and Tlacopan. The latter of these was the most modest of the three and was, in reality, little more than a Mexican colony on the lakeshore. The supremacy of the two first cities was obvious by the agreement of distribution of war booty and taxes from other villages. Two fifths were for the Mexica capital, Tenochtitlan, two for Texcoco and one for Tlacopan. On the arrival of the Spaniards, Tenochtitlan was the unquestionable leading city of the alliance.

MEXICA TEMPLE OF MALINALCO

The headless sculpture of a jaguar guards the entrance to this small teocalli.

TLACAELEL, INSPIRATION OF THE EMPIRICAL VISION

The most important figure in the birth of Mexica imperial power was Tlacaelel (1398-1480). He was the nephew of the *Tlatoani* Itzacoatl, who ascended to the position of *cihuacoatl* and was ordered to deal with the internal issues of the city. From that privileged position, avoiding that of *Tlatoani* (this position was offered to him twice and rejected) he governed the destinies of his town and reconstructed the Mexica society. As previously stated, he was the main instigator of the revolt against Azcapotzalco and the inspiration for the Triple Alliance. Heir and propagator of the imperialistic vision, warrior for his God Huitzlipochtli, he wanted to begin the new glorious destiny of his town from scratch. In the way of the Inquisitors, he proposed burning all the codices of the vassal towns in order to rewrite Mexica history and to associate them with the refined cultures of the Toltecs and the mysterious Teotihuacan. Tlacaelel established an ideology that transformed the Mexicas into guardians of the cosmic order with the militaristic, bloodthirsty god Huitzlipochtli, an essential deity for humanity's destiny, as the linchpin. Equipped with a view of the world as laid down by their God to start the new world order, the Mexicas conscientiously dedicated themselves to the construction of their empire. They had spent less than a century doing so when Cortés arrived. It will never be known what they could have achieved.

AZTEC SYMBOLS

A page from the Mendoza Codex shows the eagle on the prickly pear, symbols of the foundation of Technochtitlan. Beneath it are the shield and arrows, symbols of war. The ten people on the mats represent the clan leaders, the founders of the city.

RELIGION

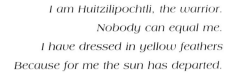

I am Huitzilipochtli, the warrior.
Nobody can equal me.
I have dressed in yellow feathers
Because for me the sun has departed.

Devotional Mexica song.

Like all Mesoamericans, the Mexicans were under the illusion that the world was destroyed cyclically and that humanity perished. According to their vision, there had been four suns that had already died and the present sun was the fifth. The destiny of the sun, like all the creatures in the cosmos, is determined on the day of its birth and, in the case of the fifth sun it was the day Nahui Ollín.

The symbol, or glifo ollín, is associated with the concept of movement and earthquakes, under which the present sun will die because of a seismic cataclysm. The Mexicans lived under the threat of the perceived fragility of their universe materializing in a fifty-two year cycle, possibly ending the world.

On this propitious day, all fires were extinguished and the inhabitants of the cities and fields waited immobile and terrified at the birth of the new day, which suggested that the sun had not stopped and that life could continue its course.

THE ORIGIN

The origin of all beings, including the Gods, is from the fundamental couple: *OmeTecuhtli*, 'the Lord of Duality' and *Omecihuatl* 'the Lady of Duality'. Over time, this couple lost importance due to their numerous offspring, a multitude of new, vigorous and active Gods. These Gods, descendants of the fundamental pair, created the world, and the first things they created were the Sun, born of sacrifice and blood. The myth says that they were all reunited in the mysterious city of Teotihuacan looking for a suitable victim to begin the creation. One of the Gods, so ugly due to leprosy, offered himself for sacrifice and decisively threw himself into the fire. From the fire rose the majestic, new and static fifth sun.

In spite of the sacrifice, the remaining Gods saw that it was essential to provide solar movement because, without it, the phenomenon, an indispensable part of life could not occur. To achieve this, the Gods offered their own blood in sacrifice, and thus the star king began his stellar day's work.

◀ THE SACRIFICES
The ritual human sacrifices, the most terrible aspect of the Mexican religion, disgusted the conquerors.

As man was directly bound to the Gods, they therefore inherited the macabre task. In order for the sun to continue its cycle and, consequently, not send humanity into darkness, it was necessary to feed the sun with *chalchihuatl*, 'the precious liquid', human blood.

The sacrifice was a holy obligation with the sun and, therefore, to man's benefit. Thanks to death, life arises. Nothing is born nor lives if it is not thanks to the blood of those sacrificed. The blood feeds the sun and, therefore, the earth, the rain, the vegetation, indeed all of nature.

THE HUMAN SACRIFICES

The great God of the Toltecs, Quetzalcoatl, was disgusted by the human sacrifices and specifically prohibited them. But the dark God Tezcatlipoca, who restored the cult of the bloodthirsty Gods, expelled him from his Tula capital. A typical sacrifice was the extraction of the live victim's heart while held down by four priests.

There were other forms of sacrifice: the beheading of women and the drowning of children to appease Tlaloc, the God of rain, while the victims sacrificed to the God of fire were thrown onto hot coals.

Normally, the victims were adorned and painted with the insignias of the God to which they were offered. Thus, they incarnated to the divinity to which they had sworn their lives at the beginning of time to save to the world. The identification of the victim with the God was

GREATER TEMPLE OF TENOCHTITLAN
The sanctuaries of Tlaloc and Huitzlipochtli, Mexican tutelary deities, are located on the superior platform.

▲

THE RITUAL SACRIFICE

Five priests hold the victim firmly while another opens the victim's chest to remove the heart.

so much so that often the victim's body was eaten in a cannibalistic ritual. These rituals were not so different to those of the Christian communion in which the body of Christ is symbolically eaten.

These human sacrifices caused a great horror among the Spaniards, convincing them that the Aztec Gods were demons holding complete power over the Indians, keeping them in hellish ignorance and depravation. These demons had to be destroyed for the sake of the souls of the Indians.

However, it was not cruelty, nor hatred, nor ethnic cleansing that inspired the Aztec sacrifices. Neither were they penal executions, nor bloody spectacles such as those carried out in ancient Rome.

Human sacrifices were the answer of Mexica society to the instability of a threatened world that required blood to continue living, so that the sun could follow its course. The sacrificial victim was not an enemy; he was the incarnation of a God that gave itself for the good of humanity.

To accept death as though it were something natural, even as a honourable culmination of life, was intrinsic to the Mexican way of thinking.

THE PRINCIPAL GODS

A feathered ball from the sky miraculously fertilized the terrestrial divinity Coatlicue, 'the one with the skirt of serpents'. The son, fruit of the virginal conception, was born armed with 'a fire serpent' that helped him to locate his numerous brothers and sisters who were the stars and the moon. This militant brother was no other than Huitzilipochtli, the principal deity of the Aztec pantheon, the burning sun of noon and God of war.

Along with Huitzilipochtli, the other deities were also of great importance to the Mexicas. A principal deity was Tezcatlipoca, God of the Great Bear, of the nocturnal sky, multiform sorcerer, and conqueror of Quetzalcoatl. There were astral divinities that were with the Gods and Goddesses of the sedentary agricultural towns of the Mexican central plateau. This is how the Mexicas accepted Tlaloc, 'the one that accumulates clouds over the mountains and brings the welcoming rain'. Tlaloc was the supreme God of the farmers and Huitzlipochtli was the God of the soldiers. Both had their temples at the peak of the great *teocalli* of Tenochtitlan. Their priests, the solar God and the rain God, were the most respected religious dignitaries.

The sun and rain, fire and water, the essential forces of nature, were equally revered in the sedentary towns built by the nomads.

Quetzalcoatl also occupied a pre-eminent place and was incorporated by the Mexicas on his arrival in the valley of Mexico where he assumed the Toltec lineage.

Another deity that gained importance was Xipe Topec (Our Skinned Lord), patron of goldsmiths and the divinity of spring and renewal. His worship was terrible. As soon as the victim died, the officiating priest would dress in his yellow-painted skin. This magical act symbolised the Earth, 'dressed with a new skin at the beginning of the rainy season', therefore originating the necessary renewal of the seasons.

THE CALENDAR

The Mesoamerican chronological system had two purposes. On one hand, it functionally set the pace for the natural changes of the stars and seasons while, on the other, it determined the destiny of each individual and his actions.

To achieve this double function required two calendars. One was named *Xihuitl*, and followed the solar year of three hundred and sixty five days, divided into eighteen months of twenty days each. Five 'empty' or 'hollow' days, considered extremely ill fated, were added during which society came to a halt. Each of the eighteen months received the name of a natural phenomenon or of the ritual corresponding to its place in the calendar. The other calendar, *Tonalpohualli* or visionary, followed the apparent orbit of Venus and came from the combination of thirteen numbers and twenty names or signs, which constituted a series of two hundred and sixty days, the duration of the visionary year. Each day was given a number and a sign in such a way that the same sign never accompanied the same number.

The dates of the solar calendar and those of the Venusians did not interfere with each other. Every day could be named according to one or other system. The Mexicans thought the sign on the day of birth would not only determine a person's life until death, but also their future destiny. This meant that a person's whole existence was under a rigorous predestination.

No Aztec, independent of his condition, would do anything without checking the signs or consulting the fortune-tellers.

The arrival of the Spaniards was foreseen via a series of signs and predictions that filled the Mexicas with fear, in particular their emperor, Moctezuma II, who, because of them began to lose his kingdom. The sovereign or *Tlatoani*, as a good Mexica, considered the signs of destiny as real as life itself. Because of this, he felt obliged to turn over his kingdom to the bearded foreigners, who were perhaps Gods related to Quetzalcoatl, who had returned to recover their throne.

The Mexican religion was an open, young religion, that was full of energy but that had not yet established an organised and coherent set of religious ideals. Its beliefs welcomed without doubt the pan-

▲

THE MEXICA CALENDAR
There were two calendars, the solar calendar of 365 days and the Venusian one of 260 days, running simultaneously. The first days of each calendar only coincided every 52 years, at which moment the Mexicans feared that the end of the world would occur.

RITUAL MASK
OF TEZCATLIPOCA
Made from a human skull covered
in semiprecious stones.

▶

SYMBOLS
OF THE AZTEC DAYS
The names, with their translation,
in order of left to right and from
top to bottom are:
Miquiztli - Death, Mazatl - Deer,
Tochtli - Rabbit,
Atl - Water, Itzcuintli - Dog,
Ozomatli - Monkey,
Malinalli - Grass,
Acatl - Cane, Ocelotl - Jaguar,
Cuauhtli - Eagle.
Cozcaquauhtli - Buzzard
Ollín - Movement
Tecpatl - Pedernal, Quiauitl - Rain,
Xochitl - Flower, Cipactli - Cayman,
Ehecatl - Wind, Calli - House,
Cuetzpallin – Iguana,
Coatl - Serpent.

▼

theon of the conquered territories. The contradictory multiplicity of nature simultaneously had its reflection in a constellation of diverse, opposed and complementary Gods. They had one or several representative Gods at all and every social level, place or activity. The religious and magical affectation was a part of every aspect of the society without forgetting anything. Religion was the structure of the Mexican civilization. Therefore, when the Spaniards destroyed this structure their civilization collapsed.

MIQUIZTLI   MAZATL   TOCHTLI   ATL   ITZCUINTLI   OZOMATLI   MALINALLI

ACATL   OCELOTL   CUAUHTLI   COZCAQUAUHTLI   OLLIN   TECPATL

QUIAUITL   XOCHTL   CIPACTLI   EHECATL   CALLI   CUETZPALLIN   COATL

THE MEXICA SOCIETY

During the time preceding the establishment and foundation of Tenochtitlan, the Mexicas were organised tribally within an essentially egalitarian society. The heads of family, the elders, jointly decided in assembly the destinies of the tribe. The heads of family - peasants-soldiers- decided in assembly the destinies of the tribe. Priesthood was the seed of a dominant class; set apart form the normal people. These were in charge of transport and taking care of the tutelary God of the tribe, Huitzilipochtli.

With the founding of the capital, Tenochtitlan, the priests maintained the social and political structures of the tribe. With time, the growth of the city combined with the economic and military growth, demanded a sophistication of the social make up. Society became hierarchical and the foundations of a city were laid and, in turn, the foundations of the future empire.

THE SOVEREIGN AND THE RULING CLASS

The town, the members of the tribe and, most certainly, the family heads elected the sovereign or *Tlatoani* (spokesman), from the verb '*tlatoa*', to speak. Meeting in a favourable place, they designated a proposed person by acclamation. Following a universal pattern, as the city grew, the electoral body became smaller. At the beginning of the 16th Century, the 'Electoral Council' was formed of one hundred people divided into five categories: *tecuhtlatoque*, thirteen great dignitaries, *ahcacauhtin*, civil servants who represented the districts of the city, the military rank and *tlenamazque* or priests of the highest rank.

The election of the *Huei Tlatoani* or 'Great Spokesman' was clearly in the hands of the oligarchy, but in the eyes of the village, the Gods had designated the sovereign. The first Aztec sovereign was Acamapichtli, a position that his son later inherited, and also his grandson followed by other members of the family. Although it appeared that the *Huei Tlatoani* was an elected position by the Council, it always passed to members of the same family and, therefore, it must be viewed as a dynasty. It was a dynasty that strove to appear as descendants of the mythical king of Tula, Quetzalcoatl, and, therefore, also of the Toltecs.

Together with the *Tlatoani*, there were other dignitaries, normally relatives of the sovereign. Among them was the *Cihuacoatl*, 'The Serpent Woman', a kind of prime minister. She was the supreme judge for the military as well as for politics and legality. She organised the military expeditions and appointed the commanders. She stood in for the sovereign during his absences and summoned the Electoral Council on the death of *Tlatoani*, being highly regarded until the appointment of the next one. She was only inferior in dignity and sovereignty to *Tlatoani*.

HOME LIFE

Housework was exclusively for women. They were also in charge of textiles.

▼

Within the denomination of *Tecuhtli*, dignitaries or gentleman, were the principal commanders of the armies, the high-ranking civil servants, the heads of the districts of the capital *(Calpulli)*, and the superior magistrates.

The sovereigns of the tributary towns were also *Tecuhtli*, as was the emperor or *Tlatoani*.

It could be said that *Tecuhtli* was composed of the nobility, although its status was not hereditary. Any citizen could ascend to the social category of *Tecuhtli* by virtue of military achievements or public service. The position and privileges of *Tecuhtli* could not be inherited they had to be earned. This structure, based on merit and

Marriages did not occur without the intervention of matchmakers. The two people were united by the tying the ends of their cloaks during a ceremony attended by the respective families and the members of the clans.

not inheritance, guaranteed social dynamism, thus avoiding stagnation. In spite of this, the *Tecuhtli* wanted to perpetuate their status so that their children could not return to be*macehualli*, 'plebeians'. At birth they were given the title of *Pilli*, 'Son of *Tecuhtli*', which already carried some hereditary privileges. They were educated in *calmecac*, or superior schools to those of the districts and the emperor selected the judges and high civil employees from these schools.

The *Pilli*, nevertheless, were under an obligation to undertake commendable acts to ascend to *Tecuhtli* and to be able to pass to their children the status of *Pilli*. This status was not transferred beyond one generation, but had to be re-activated through new services.

As well as governors of the cities and places, the other high-ranking civil servants were the *Calpixque*, in charge of administration and collection of taxes. The judges ensured *'they were not alcoholics, corrupt or were acceptors of people nor passionate'.*

THE PRIESTS

All the young *Pilli* were educated in *calmecac*, a type of monastic school where they shared their lives with the priests. Although, supposedly, the *calmecac* schools were only for the young *Pilli*, in fact any member of society, retailer or plebeian, could be accepted in the sacerdotal career if he showed the aptitude for it. Quetzalcoatl was the divinity to which the priests devoted themselves. Any student who, by the age of twenty, did not leave the *calmecac* to marry, was accorded the title of *tlamacazqui*, or priest.

The more experienced priests that ascended the hierarchy could get to be *tlenamacac* and, therefore, be a part of the Electoral Council of *Tlatoani*.

The hierarchic summit of the Mexican church was bicephalous and comprised two ecclesiastics, *Quetzalcoatl Totec tlamatazqui*, 'Feathered Serpent Priest of our Lord', of the Huitzlipochtli cult, and *Quetzalcoatl Tlaloc tlamacazqui*, 'Feathered Serpent Priest of Tlaloc'. The multiplicity and complexity of the religious rites demanded a multitude of priests who, along with the civil servants and the soldiers, comprised the ruling classes.

THE *CALPULLI*

The *calpulli* was a territory owned by a group of families who shared their land. The original Mexican tribe was made up of seven *calpulli* and was based there. With time, the *calpulli* became the suburbs of the capital, each one with its own temple and school, or *telpochcalli*.

The head of the suburb, or *calpulli*, was a *Calpullec*, chosen by the members of the clan with the agreement of the sovereign. A group of elderly men, or *huehuetque*, advised the Capullec. His mission was, in

▲

THE CELEBRATIONS

*Despite of the fatalistic nature of
Mexican society, the people did
not miss an opportunity to have
fun on any of the events indicated
in their calendars. The illustration
shows knights of the orders of the
Eagle and the Jaguar in the
celebrations at the coronation of
Moctezuma II.*

essence, 'to protect and to defend his fellow citizens' through administrative, representative and military functions, because the Aztec armies were organised according to the structure of the clans of *calpulli.*

Calpulli, with his *calpullec* and advisers, was the basis of Mexican society.

The young people were educated in *telpochcalli*, 'the houses of the young people', of each suburb, which they entered at the age of six or seven. Their tutelary God was Tezcatlipoca and the education was essentially religious and military. As will be seen later, all men born in the Mexica society were predestined for war.

A CLASS APART: THE *POCHTECS* OR MERCHANTS

The small subsistence traders, like farmers and fishermen, did not form their own class. The *pochtecs* were members of the powerful organizations that had the monopoly of foreign trade. They organised the carriers that linked the capital with both coasts, the Pacific and the Gulf of Mexico.

The Mexicans purchased the raw materials with the taxes they collected from cities and towns. For that reason, the products exported by the *pochtecs* were manufactured in Mexico: fabrics, leather, rugs and feathers, obsidian knives, dyes and perfumes, and they imported exotic, luxury items such as jade, marine emeralds, sea snails, jaguar and puma skins, as well as amber and quetzal feathers.

Trade was not an accepted activity of a tribal, nomadic or warlike society. The Aztecs from the conquered cities adopted the institution of the unions of retailers such as the *pochteca*. These unions were lead by a small group of elderly men who represented their sovereign as well as being responsible for distributing justice between those of their class. This was a unique situation in Aztec society.

The *pochteca* were different, they had their own suburbs, laws, gods, cults and rituals that they conducted without priests. They

THE MEXICA UPPER CLASS
*Representation of a priest, Tecuhtli
and an Aztec princess.*

could accumulate wealth, although it was specifically prohibited for them to flaunt it. It would be fair to say that they were the equivalent of modern middle class.

Nevertheless, they did not escape the military or warrior vision as their commercial expeditions were also missions of exploration and intelligence gathering for the military leaders.

'We, the *pochtec, put our heads and lives at risk, and we work night and day but, although we are call ourselves merchants and we seem as though we are, we are captains and soldiers who march towards conquest.'*

THE CRAFTSMEN, THE MASSES AND THE SLAVES

The Aztec craftsmen formed an abundant class and, as with the medieval European craftsmen, they had their own suburbs and institutions.

The chronicles emphasize the importance of the craftsmen of luxury items, such as goldsmiths, jewellers and the feather weavers, who were essential for the imperial decoration. The latter wove the cloaks, headdresses and feather bedspreads that elicited much admiration from the Spaniards by their exoticism and perfection.

The factories were family based. The men wove the feathers, the women embroidered and dyed, while the children learned the trade.

The craftsmen were also called Toltecs, and enjoyed privileges such as the exemption of the tributary personal work.

THE MEXICA TOWN

The illustration shows a Pochtec, *a farmer or* macehualli, *and a slave.*

The Aztec word *'tecuhtlimacehualli'* means 'worker' and was for those that we would call plebeians, the peasants of the population.

However, they were citizens with full rights because they belonged to the tribe, which brought with it unavoidable obligations.

They had the right to work on a block of land where they could build a house. All the children were educated in the schools in the suburb and they participated completely in the social and religious life and could also receive aid from the public purse if necessary. In addition, if they were intelligent and brave they could ascend socially by military merit.

This was linked to their main obligation, military service, which was compulsory and was considered an honour and a religious duty. As throughout the rest of the Old World, they were the class that paid the taxes, from either the products of their fields or by manual work, participating in public works of urban development.

The *tlacotli*, were considered neither citizens nor people but slaves. They were viewed as an object belonging to their master. However, slavery in Mexico was not as terrible as in the rest of the world. The *tlacotli* could intermarry with free citizens and their off-spring were not born slaves but were free. They had many opportunities to redeem their freedom, for instance through the death of their master, by imperial decree or by purchase. Slavery was not a definitive state, it could be a temporary stage in a person's life. In fact, the majority of the slaves were volunteers; helpless, lazy people unable to get on in life without selling themselves as slaves.

THE MARCH TO WAR

The Tlatoani Aztecs leaving for war receiving gestures of respect from their people.

THE WAR

The War was sacred because it gave meaning to their existence and gave direction to the city's energy. Where else could they obtain the precious blood the sun needed if the universe wasn't to be condemned to destruction? As the Aztec Empire expanded, there were no problems obtaining prisoners for the sacrifices on the altars. However, with time, it was realised that it was absurd to continue having permanent enemy cities.

The ritual and sacred concept of war led them to devise the 'Flower War' that consisted of the organising of limited battles. The opposing armies met at a pre-determined place and date, as was the way of the medieval European battles. The soldiers displayed their fighting skills in ceremonial form, although they could be wounded with consideration.

The troops on the defeated side became sacrificial victims. The priests were present at the battles and brought them to a halt when sufficient men had been captured.

As well as the sacred concept of the war, there was also a cosmic relevance. The traditional vision of the average war was of conquest and the submission of other towns for the sake of imperial expansion, *'Because the three heads, Tenochtitlán, the Texcoco and Tlacopan, were based on being lords and masters over all the rest, by the right which they aspired over all the land which had belonged to the Toltecs and of whom they were the successors and heirs.'*

THE MILITARY CAREER

The supreme head of the army was the emperor, or *Tlatoani*, who was given the title of *Tlacatecuhtli*, 'Lord of the Men'. Four officials, or generals, who were usually members of his family, assisted him in his military functions. They were in charge of the four contingents provided by *calpulli* from the four sectors of Tenochtitlan.

The two most important were *Tlacateccatl*, 'Lord of the Soldiers' and *Tlacachcalcatl* 'Lord of the House of the Darts', presumably the person in charge of armament and the arsenals.

In Tenochtitlan, all men whatever their situation, were or had been soldiers. From birth, the men were destined for war. The umbilical cord of the newborn was buried next to a miniature bow and arrows.

In the *telpochcalli*, or suburban schools, the young people were educated so that their main aspiration was to distinguish themselves in battle. The first feat of the young soldier consisted of capturing a prisoner, although he needed the help of some companions for this.

From that moment he held the title of *iyac*. However, despite this, if he fought in two or three battles without any significant achievement, he would be forced to resign his arms and to turn his attention to the fields and the family, which was the normal life of a plebeian or *macehualli*.

If, on the other hand, he had been born under a lucky star, he continued his military career until he captured four enemies in combat. Then he would reach the level of *tequitl*, and accede to a superior category that allowed him to receive pay or part of the taxes. In addition, he could participate in the advising of the soldiers and could wear feathers and bracelets, the symbols of a great soldier. If he distinguished himself exceptionally in battle he would be admitted into one of the two military orders, the jaguar horsemen, soldiers of Tezcatlipoca or the eagle horsemen, soldiers of the sun.

Soldiers who proved themselves in battle enjoyed great privileges. However, it must not be forgotten that all the wealth and honours were obtained through their heroic deeds.

To die in combat or on the sacrificial altar was the highest honour to aspire to because it guaranteed social recognition and the promise of eternal happiness.

The Battle

The armies organised themselves according to the clans and their corresponding *calpulli* of the capital. The generals were prominent because they were carried on platforms that were magnificently decorated with coloured feathers.

Before the start of the battle, the soldiers let out deafening shouts, supported by the howls of the shells, the beating of drums and the high-pitched sound of bone whistles. The musical instruments served not only to uplift the soldiers and intimidate the enemy, but were also used by the commanders to relay orders.

Next, the archers and stone-throwers released their missiles and the soldiers went into battle with their clubs and shields. As soon as the battle began, the hand-to-hand combat was different from any other in the world.

The Aztec soldier did not try to kill or injure his opponent but tried to capture them alive. Squires accompanied the soldiers and carried ropes to immobilise the enemy once they had been defeated.

The battle turned into a multitude of duels or small combats with each side trying to capture the other. The objective of the war was to capture as many live enemies as possible as potential sacrifices to the Gods, but obviously the defeat of the enemy army was also desired, with the exception of the flower wars. A city was declared defeated when the attackers managed to break into the temple and set the local God's sanctuary on fire.

THE MILITARY ORDERS ▶
Knight of the Military Order of the Jaguar, the elite warriors in the Mexicas army.

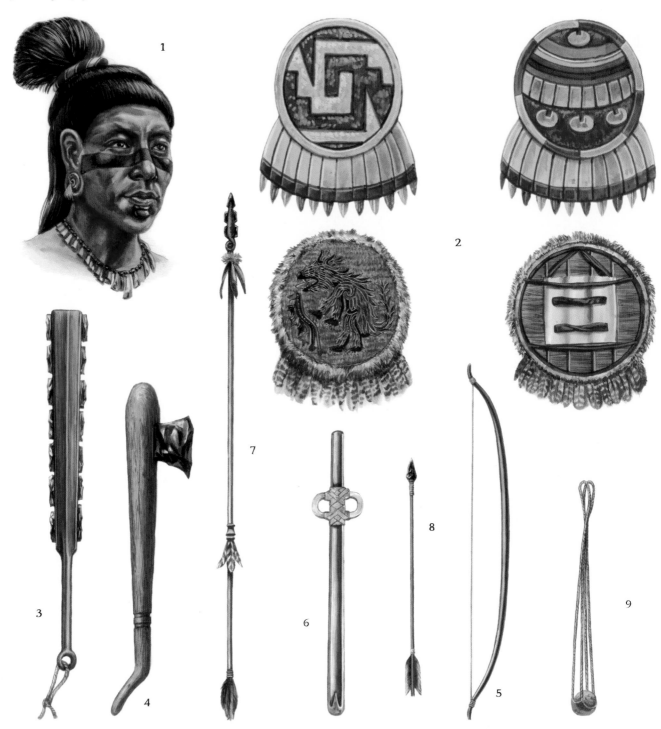

ARMAMENT

The basic armament of the Mexican warrior (1) consisted of a round shield, *chimalli* (2), made of wood or cane and covered with feathers or fabrics painted with the colours of the clan, and a *macquahuitl* wooden club (3). This was the most effective weapon as it was encrusted with sharpened obsidian blades. The Mexican warriors looked upon it as their most dangerous weapon, but it proved ineffective against Spanish armour. The war axe (4) was also made of wood with a sharpened obsidian blade.

The bow, or *tlautiolli* (5), was a Toltec weapon used by the Aztecs, but it was not as accurate or as robust as the European bows.

The *atlatl* thrower (6) could project arrows (*mitl*) (7) or javelins (*tlacohtli*) (8).

A weapon that caused most damage to the Spaniards was the sling (9) that came from the matlaltzincas of the Toluca valley. The half-wild chinantecs from the mountains of Oaxaca used lances with stone points (10).

As armour or body protection they wore the *ichcaupilli* (11), a tunic of quilted cotton or a vest hardened with brine. The helmets had a decorative, prestigious and distinct function. They were made of wood, extravagantly decorated with feathers, paper or colourful zoomorphic figures.

The everyday clothes worn by the peasants consisted of the *maxtlatl* or loincloth and the multi-purpose *tilmatli* or cloak, which also served as a coverlet, awning or clothing. Veteran soldiers wore fitted suits with sleeves and trousers (12) that clearly distinguished them from the others. These suits could be multi-coloured, either associated with the wearer's clan or to their personal taste, except those of the Jaguar knight (13). These were made from Jaguar skin while those of the Eagle knight (14) were covered with eagle feathers.

The banners and flags (15) that the commanders tied to their backs were very important in the battle, as well as for the organization and training of the armies. These were made of cane because of its light weight, and were decorated with multi-coloured feathers, jewels and gold. Documentation shows that the Mexicas were very imaginative when designing the banners. Figures of different birds, especially birds of prey, parasols and feathered fans were used. It appears that any design was valid as long as it was bright, clearly distinguishable and multi-coloured. In accordance with the aforementioned regulations, it should be understood that only those who were distinguished for military merit used the banners and adornments. The inappropriate use of such items was severely punished.

Moctezuma Xocoyotzin
(1480-1520)

He was the Huei Tlatoani who governed the empire upon the arrival of the Spaniards. One of the Spanish soldiers, Bernal Díaz del Castillo, described him thus: 'the great Moctezuma was around forty years of age, tall and well built, slender, not very sallow, but with the natural tones of an Indian. His hair was not worn long and his beard was thin and neatly groomed. His face was quite long but jolly. He was very neat and clean and bathed twice a day, in the afternoon.

He was quite a womanizer, with lovers who were daughters of political leaders and two legitimate wives.

He didn't wear the same clothes within any four-day period. He had two hundred political leaders in his guard and when they went to speak with him, they had to take off their luxurious cloaks and put on others of less value. They also had to be barefoot and with eyes downcast, as they were not permitted to look him in the face. And they bowed to him three times'.

MOCTEZUMA XOCOYOTZIN, THE LAST MEXICAN SOVEREIGN
Moctezuma surrounded by warriors and labourers, the basis of the imperial army. Next to him are two warriors from the two military orders, the Jaguar and the Eagle.

BAD OMENS

*The omens announced the end
of the Mexica culture.
Moctezuma, from the terrace of
his palace, observed a comet
that, in the Aztec religion, was
an especially disastrous omen.*

THE MEXICAN EMPIRE AND THE ARRIVAL OF CORTES

When the Spaniards arrived in Mexico, the Mexica Empire was at the peak of its power. While it did not have a solid imperial structure, nothing could have predicted the quick collapse that followed. The last sovereign, Moctezuma Xocoyotzin, had extended his legacy and collected taxes from three hundred and seventy one cities.

However, the Aztec empire was not entirely like the Inca, they did not claim ownership of the land, the world or the people. They did not impose an exclusive language and culture. It was more of a flexible confederation of city-states and tributaries of Tenochtitlan, who were free to carry out their own policies.

The Mexicans only required that the superiority of their God Huitzilipochtli be universally recognised. Their intention was not to cause the decline of the country or to kill the population. Once the pre-eminence of the Mexica god was established, there was no reason for war. All that remained was to set the taxes for the defeated by means of bargaining and negotiations. The defeated city was allowed to maintain its institutions, rituals, customs and language.

The city, in this case Tenochtitlan, was the focal point for ideas and the central base for the armies. It was also where the taxes were sent. It was the commercial and religious centre, the base of the state. In fact, the ideas of the state hardly went beyond the city.

How many inhabitants did Tenochtitlan have? It is estimated that there would have been around one hundred thousand homes, taking into account that many lived permanently on the boats. Families were numerous and essentially monogamous. Polygamy was a prerogative of the rul-

SANCTUARIES AND RITUALS
The sanctuaries, or chapels of Tlaloc and Huitzilipochtli and Tzompantli, contain a collection of skulls of the sacrificed.

ing classes. Also, it was normal to possess slaves. So, establishing this figure as a basis, it is possible that the population would have consisted of around five hundred thousand inhabitants, an enormous figure when compared to any contemporary European city. In addition, there were also suburbs, cities and villages located around Texcoco Lake and the great city's workers who commuted each day. By taking these into account, the number of inhabitants increases dramatically.

In fact, scholars are in agreement that Mesoamerica was densely populated before the arrival of the Spaniards, and believed the population to be around fifteen million. The smallpox and measles epidemics, imported from Europe, were devastating; causing an apocalyptic loss of life that reduced the inhabitants to less than two million by 1581.

INTERNAL DISSENT

Within the tributary territories of Tenochtitlan, a number of independent cities existed that did not come under the sway of the Mexicas. The most famous of these cities was Tlaxcala. According to the Aztec chronicles, the Mexicas did not want to conquer this city in order to continue the necessary wars to obtain victims for the altars. The Tlaxaltecs reasons were different. For them the war was about survival, they hated Tenochtitlan and they fought for their freedom. Consequently, they did not hesitate to form an alliance with Cortés against the Aztecs. This alliance was vital for the Spaniards because it provided native warriors, supplies, information and refuge when necessary.

By the time the Spaniards arrived, the city of Tenochtitlan clearly dominated the empire. Tlacopan, one of the cities of the Triple Alliance, had been totally absorbed and Texcoco was on the same path. In 1515, the sovereign of Texcoco died and Moctezuma did not hesitate to give the throne to *Tlatoani*, son of a tenochcan, which was clearly in line with his interests. This situation was a cause of irritation to the Texcocano prince, Ixtlilxochitl, who considered himself heir to the Texcoco throne. As the sworn enemy of the Mexicas, he also allied himself to the Spaniards, supplying them with troops, workers and connections.

As is obvious, the weakness of the Aztec state, although under threat from a number of directions, would not have collapsed on its own, at least in the short term, given the military strength of Tenochtitlan. This weakness was only one advantage used by the Spanish conquistadores. When Tezcatlipoca expelled Quetzalcoatl, he announced his return for the year *Ce-Acatl* that, in the Aztec calendar, could fall either in 1363, 1467 or 1519, the year Cortés landed in Mexico.

THE STATE OF THE SPANISH CROWN

Throughout most of the 15th Century, the Iberian Kingdoms were devastated by numerous civil wars. Spanish unity was a mere fiction kept alive by a few nostalgic Spaniards, predominantly from the Christian Visigoth kingdoms.

Apart from the multiple dynastic conflicts between the Christian kings and the nobles, the Nasrid kingdom of Granada continued to look back to the centuries of Muslim occupation. On the death, in 1410, of the heirless King, Martín I of Aragon, at the time the regent of Castile, assumed Aragon's crown. Ferdinand of Antequera strengthened the ties binding the Trastamara ruling families of two of the Peninsula's most powerful kingdoms, Castile and Aragon. The dream of unity began to take shape with the marriage between the cousins Isabella and Ferdinand in 1469, who were heirs to the previously mentioned crowns and future Catholic monarchs. However, it was not to be an easy undertaking. The two young royals had to demonstrate their intelligence and fortitude in order to prove their suitability to succeed to the throne. Specifically, Isabella had to defend her dynastic rights to the Castilian crown in a civil war against her opponents, supported by the Portuguese king. In 1479, Ferdinand was crowned King of Aragon and, at least in name, the two crowns were united although, in practice, they were two separate kingdoms. Aragon and Castile maintained separate institutions, customs and currencies and conserved their own identity and legal norms. The state of the two kingdoms was very different. Castile exercised demographic strength and a strong economy, trading wool and raw materials with the Netherlands. Aragon, on the other hand, was in a different situation due to the dispersed power of its nobility and its disparate nationalities: Catalonian, Valencian, Balearic and Italian. Also, the institution of the Royal courts evolved differently in both kingdoms. In Castile, they were losing representation. The clergy and nobility ceased being summoned and the few cities that were called were represented by local oligarchies. The courts of Aragon, on the contrary, continued to be strong and defended their local jurisdictions and, even during Philip II's reign, they upheld their interests against the powerful monarchy.

POLICY OF ISABELLA AND FERDINAND

Despite the differences between the two kingdoms, the Catholic monarchs, Isabella and Ferdinand, shared the modern idea of strengthening the monarchy and the state while acting against the

◀ *THE RETURN OF THE EXPLORER*
Christopher Columbus is received by the Catholic Monarchs on his return from his first voyage of discovery.

THE PENINSULAR KINGDOMS
Although the Iberian kingdoms,
with the exception of Portugal,
were united under the one crown,
in reality they continued to exercise
a great deal of legal and economic
autonomy.

▼

power of the nobility and clergy. Intelligent and dynamic, both practically assumed the total running of the government, awarding administrative positions to civil employees, thus undermining the nobles. They also placed the ecclesiastical hierarchy under their authority, reserving the right to propose the candidates for the Spanish bishopric.

Everything they undertook during their reign was aimed at the creation of a strong, unified state that was able to play an important role in European politics. To this end, they incited the conquest of the last Muslim bastion in the Peninsula, the kingdom of Granada. During the long, drawn-out, exhausting campaign, Aragonese and Castilian knights fought side-by-side thus strengthening their Christian bond in the fight against the Infidel.

Fomenting this Christian bond seemed essential to the Catholic Monarchs in their fight to unite a kingdom, where three different religions had coexisted for eight centuries. To this end, they established the Spanish Inquisition in Spain, a medieval European institution that was very useful for the crown's policy. The Inquisition operated freely throughout the peninsular kingdoms, eliminating heresy and heretics and, indeed, any behaviour believed to be in opposition to the integrating interests of the monarchs. Within this policy, in 1492, following the examples of France and England, they ordered the expulsion of the Jews from its kingdoms. However, many Jews preferred to remain in Sefarad, the name they gave to Spain, becoming

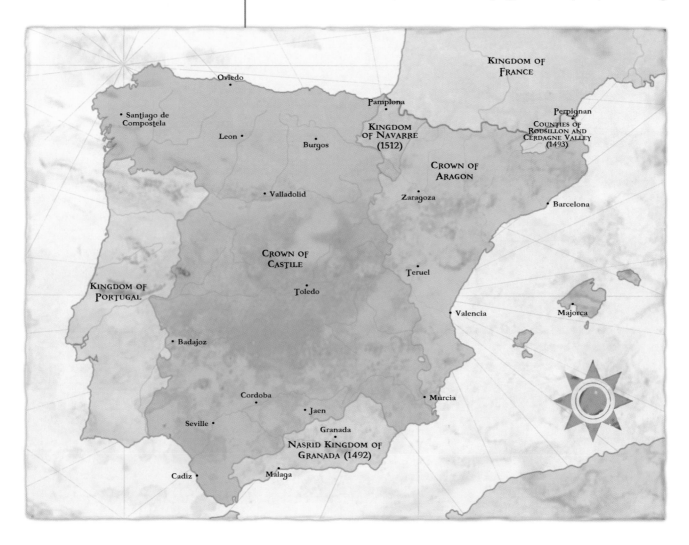

JUANA LA LOCA

Queen Joanna of Castile, mother of Emperor Charles, had to be incarcerated in the Castilian town of Tordesillas because of her mental problems.

Christians. This gave origin to the problem of the converted Jews and the cleansing of blood that poisoned Spanish society for almost three centuries. The Inquisition combed every corner of society in search of the false converted Jews while, at the same time, it demanded a clean bloodline, free of any Jewish or Moorish blood, before any person was able to gain a public position and/or social recognition.

The discovery of the New World marked a new path in the history of Spain. However, in the years leading up to the end of the 15th century, the new continent was rather a future value than a reality. At that time, only a few islands inhabited by half-wild Indians had been discovered and there were just a few new territories open to colonization and little more.

Meanwhile, Ferdinand's attention was soon absorbed with problems in Italy and the necessity to defend the Aragonese house of Naples against Charles VIII of France.

The Spanish army, already fully battle-hardened following its campaigns in Granada, reached military perfection during the Italian campaigns under the command of the 'Great Captain', Gonzalo Fernández de Córdoba, creator of the formidable Spanish infantry that commanded the European battlefields for the next 150 years.

Fernández de Córdoba gave preference to the early firearms, called harquebus, in place of the heavy cavalry. He aligned his troops, organised under 'Capitanías' of 250 men divided into 'Tercios' (thirds) composed of pike-men, harquebusiers and crossbowmen and a last one of sword-and-buckler men.

Justly proud of his Italian triumphs, Ferdinand 'The Catholic' ordered his army to join in battle against the kingdom of Navarre that became part of the crown of Castile in 1512.

THE YOUNG EMPEROR ▲

*At the moment of the conquest,
King Charles was named Emperor
at the tender age of twenty.*

COLUMBUS' FIRST VOYAGE

*The route taken by Columbus on
his voyage to discover America
suggested knowledge of the trade
winds that, in theory, nobody in
the world could know.*

▼

THE INHERITANCE OF THE CATHOLIC MONARCHS

While peninsular unity appeared almost a fact, it continued to have fragile foundations. The Catholic Monarchs' policy of promoting the marriages of the Spanish princesses with the European ruling houses had unexpected results.

After the premature deaths of Prince John, his older sister, Isabella, and the grandson of the Catholic Monarchs, Prince Michael, succession to the Spanish kingdoms fell to Princess Joanna and her husband Philip 'The Handsome', son of the Emperor Maximilian I, who inherited Castile in 1504, following the death of Queen Isabella.

To prevent the loss of the Aragonese crown to his mad daughter Joanna, and her unpleasant husband, Philip, Ferdinand quickly remarried. However, fate also lent a hand when Philip and the new-born son of Ferdinand and Germaine of Foix both died. This resulted, on the death of the Old Catholic king, in the crowns of Castile and Aragon being handed to a young Flemish prince. He had been educated abroad and spoke no Castilian nor knew the customs of his new kingdom. Charles, the future King, was the son of Joanna and Philip and, therefore, grandson of the Holy Roman Emperor Maximilian. Upon Charles' arrival in Spain, surrounded by his Flemish advisors, it was confirmed that his mother Joanna would be shut away in Tordesillas, reigning only as a figurehead.

The Castilians distrustfully watched their new monarch. This distrust soon resulted in open rebellion when it was discovered that his primary interest in the Spanish kingdoms was to collect sufficient funds to allow him access to the Holy Germanic Empire. Young Charles left Spain and, by way of payment of a substantial sum of money, asserted his right of succession to the Holy Roman Empire among the German voters.

A wave of uprisings spread throughout the kingdom, mainly headed by the Castilian cities. Only Burgos remained loyal to the monarch because of its important commercial bonds with the Flemish countries. The Comuneros (supporters of the 'Communities' in Castile)

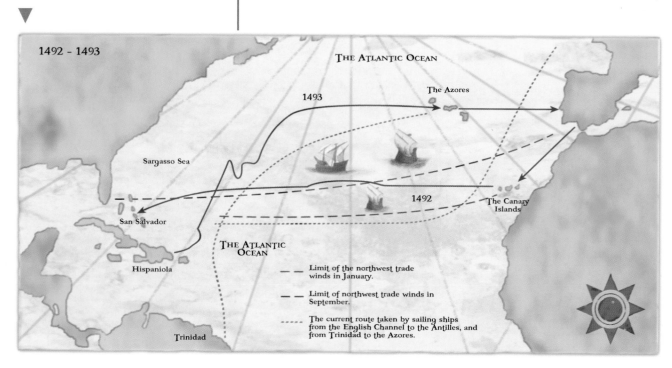

1492 - 1493

THE ATLANTIC OCEAN

1493

The Azores

Sargasso Sea

1492

The Canary Islands

San Salvador

THE ATLANTIC OCEAN

Hispaniola

Limit of the northwest trade winds in January.

Limit of northwest trade winds in September.

The current route taken by sailing ships from the English Channel to the Antilles, and from Trinidad to the Azores.

Trinidad

THE SPANISH INFANTRY
AT THE CLOSE
OF THE 15TH CENTURY
On the left a harquebusier, a
drummer and a crossbowman. On
the right two harquebusiers and a
sword-and-buckler man.

'EL GRAN CAPITAN'
Gonzalo Fernández of Córdoba
views the corpse of his enemy, the
Duke of Nemours, defeated in the
battle of Cerignola (1503) during
the campaigns of Italy.

rebellion was bound to fail when Queen Joanna refused to support the movement against her son Charles. With this paucity of legal support and with the nobility switching over to the royal side, the citizens and Comunera militia were defeated by the royal army at Villalar. Along with the Comuneros´ flags, the independence of Castile also fell, and from that moment on it was forced to support the policies of the Hapsburg Empire. In Valencia and Majorca, the winds of rebellion also blew with craftsmen and small retailers demanding a greater representation in the municipal governments. This initial urban revolt also extended to the peasantry but, as in Castile, it was quickly crushed by an alliance between the nobility and the high clergy, backed by the Imperial armies. This all happened while Hernán Cortés was busy conquering Mexico.

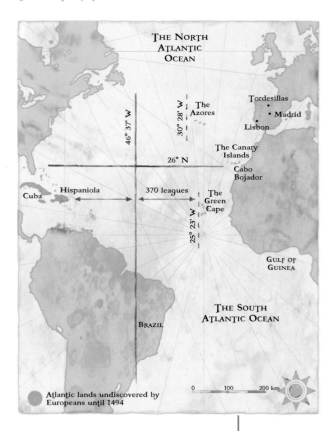

THE NORTH
ATLANTIC
OCEAN

46° 37' W

30° 28' W

The
Azores

Tordesillas
• Madrid

Lisbon

The Canary
Islands

26° N

Cabo
Bojador

Hispaniola   370 leagues   The
Green
Cape

Cuba

25° 23' W

GULF OF
GUINEA

THE SOUTH
ATLANTIC OCEAN

BRAZIL

Atlantic lands undiscovered by
Europeans until 1494

0   100   200 km

THE TREATY
OF TORDESILLAS

By this treaty, signed in 1494,
Spain and Portugal shared the
overseas rights of discovery and
conquest.

POPE ALEXANDER IV ▶

The Pontiff, Rodrigo Borgia,
legitimised the Treaty of Tordesillas
favouring Castilian interests.

THE NEW WORLD COLONIES

At the beginning of the 16th century, Spain occupied a predominant place in the European panorama. With its unified and consolidated kingdoms, it was the principal link between the newly discovered continent, rich in possibilities, and old Europe. It only had one rival in the race of the Discoveries, the kingdom of Portugal. Castile, the major promoter of Columbus' expeditions, to the detriment of Aragon, required legal and moral backing to justify its colonial expansion. For this, Castile counted on the invaluable support of Pope Alexander VI, the infamous Rodrigo Borgia from Valencia.

In 1494 the Treaty of Tordesillas was signed between Spain and Portugal. It was the first time in history that two European powers shared the known world for their own exploitation. Under the pact, any possible territorial disputes with Portugal were eliminated, by dividing the globe with a meridian crossing the Atlantic. America was for the Spaniards, thus leaving the road free for the Portuguese in the future Brazil, given that the meridian cut through South America at its most easterly point.

THE FIRST DISCOVERIES

The colonial administration was under the direction by two institutions, the Council of the Indies, responsible for the administrative work, and the House of Hiring in Seville. This southern Spanish city and port on the Guadalquivir River became one of the most important commercial ports in Europe as it held the privilege of the trade monopoly with the Indies. All merchandise and people arriving from America had, unavoidably, to pass through Seville. The discovery was a private venture, financed by the members of the expedition. The troops went without pay, with the promise that they would receive recompense from what was obtained from the conquered land, including precious metals and jewels, Indians or the land itself. Only the mates received a salary as it was assumed that

▲

THE TRADE MONOPOLY
The port of Seville held the
monopoly of trade with the Indies
until the 18th Century.

they could not go ashore to discover and colonize, as they had to remain on board and take care of the ships. The Crown was limited to provide the essential legal cover.

Before 1518, almost the entire east coast of the Americas had been seen. The discovery had sighted from the Gulf of Honduras to the south of the mouth of the River Plate. Balboa had crossed the jungle on the Panamanian isthmus and discovered the Pacific Ocean. The Bahamas, the Caribbean Islands and the Florida Peninsula had been explored. Nevertheless, the borders of the Gulf of Mexico remained unknown. Cuba was the second most important island to be discovered although, during Columbus' lifetime, it was yet to be colonized. In 1511, when Nicholas de Ovando was the Spanish governor, he prepared a small force, under the command of Diego Velázquez, to conquer and colonize Cuba. Diego Velázquez was to play a very important role in the later conquest of Mexico.

Following the Cuban conquest, Velázquez was appointed governor of the island and, making use of this position, he very quickly colonized it, founding establishments and founding the capital in Santiago in the south-eastern angle of the island.

The colonization was carried out by means of 'division', through which the conquistadores were granted a given number of Indians to work their land or 'encomiendas, (the encomienda was a repressive system fixing the Spanish conquistadores' entitlement to labour and tribute from Indian communities. Although the Indians, theoretically, remained free subjects of the Spanish Crown, in practice they were enslaved to the 'encomenderos', those having encomienda rights). This system gave way to innumerable cruelties, because the indigenous people, unused to hard labour because of the boundless generosity of the islands, were faced with the pressures of the cruel encomenderos. Thousands of Indians died from imported diseases (smallpox, influenza and measles), and by their intensive work as slaves in the mines.

Only the Catholic Church raised its voice against this injustice with Friar Bartolomé de las Casas as their principal defender. Las Casas argued that the Indians were innocent creatures, confused by the devil, but they were still God's children, and had to be led into Christ's light. As God's children they were free and under no circumstances could they be enslaved.

THE EXPEDITION OF HERNÁNDEZ DE CÓRDOBA

Hernández of Córdoba arrived on the Yucatan peninsula after being blown there during a storm. When news of the Mayan civilization reached Cuba, the governor became avaricious.

▼

This vision, defended so passionately by the friar, created a moral problem in the home country, as it had never before been raised in other colonial empires. The morality of the conquest and the consequent exploitation of the Indians were questioned. The Crown laid down a law that specifically prohibited the enslaving of the indigenous people. However, this law was, more or less, given a blind eye due to the urgent requirement for labour for the mining and agricultural work in the colonies. Over time, the necessity for native slavery was replaced when black slaves began to be imported from Africa. By then, the islands' native population had practically been wiped out.

THE EXPEDITIONS OF HERNÁNDEZ DE CÓRDOBA AND JUAN DE GRIJALVA

The expeditions, which would eventually lead to the conquest of Tenochtitlan, set sail from Santiago de Cuba. Hernández de Córdoba was a Cuban hidalgo who departed the city on the 8th February 1517 and headed towards the Bahamas in search of Indian slaves. Tropical storms forced him off course and he put into port on the Yucatan peninsula. The Spaniards were amazed to see the first signs of a citizen civilization in the New World, buildings and sophisticated crops. However, the inhabitants, the Mayans, had already received news of the depredations of the bearded foreigners, this being the reason why Córdoba and his men were received with the utmost hostility when they disembarked.

Exhausted, injured and decimated, the Spaniards returned to Cuba where their reports convinced the governor Velázquez of the necessity of preparing a new venture.

This time, command of the expedition fell upon his nephew Juan de Grijalva, an honest, simple, prudent man of proven loyalty to the governor. The fleet set sail from Santiago de Cuba on the 1st May of 1518. Initially, they sailed the same course as Hernández of Córdoba, arriving at the same destinations and, like their predecessors, the Grijalva's Spaniards were impressed by the architecture. Something must have reminded Grijalva of his native peninsula for he decided to name the discovered territories 'Nueva España'. A name that later extended from the Yucatan peninsula to cover all of Mexico.

The indigenous people continued to give them a hostile reception, but eventually Grijalva made contact with a chief who gave them a rich gift of jewels and gold

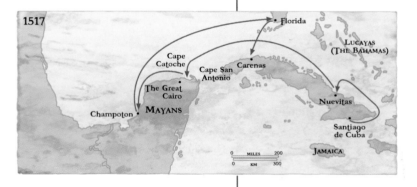

GRIJALVA'S EXPEDITION

Grijalva's expedition set sail from Cuba with the intention of exploring the continent and compiling information. The gold obtained made Governor Velázquez decide to charter a third and final expedition.

▶

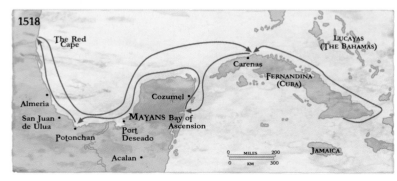

BARTOLOMÉ DE LAS CASAS
This monk dedicated his life
fighting for the rights of the
Indians; he succeeded in forcing
the Spanish Crown in passing a
law forbidding native slavery.

adornments. The local chief probably wanted to thoroughly observe the foreigners to be able to send information about them to his master Moctezuma. Grijalva rejected a proposal by his men to found a colony in that place, and commanded one of his captains, Pedro de Alvarado, to return to Cuba with the treasure and the information that there was a powerful inland kingdom.

Grijalva's orders were to trade with the Indians and to collect information. To this end, he continued the exploration of the coast and, after passing San Juan de Ulua; he encountered headwinds on the same latitude as Cabo Rojo, forcing him to return to Cuba six months after his departure.

On his return to the island, he was surprised to find out that a much more powerful military expedition was being chartered to continue the exploration of the continent. The information and the gold brought by Alvarado had excited the greed of the governor. Control of the expedition was taken away from Juan de Grijalva and he was accused of being faint hearted, as he hadn't wanted to found a colony on the land. This was an unjust accusation, as the honest Grijalva had limited himself to following his orders. Upon Velázquez receiving the Royal Court's permission to continue with the exploration and colonization of the new land, he sought a captain for his fleet. He choice fell on the young Hernán Cortés, mayor of Santiago de Cuba and joint financer of the expedition.

THE OSUNA CODEX OF THE
GOVERNORS 1563
Despite the laws protecting the
native population, they were
forced to work in the fields and
mines owned by the Spanish
agents.

THE CONQUISTADORES

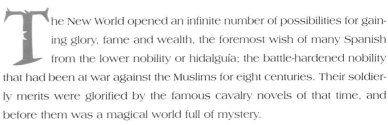he New World opened an infinite number of possibilities for gaining glory, fame and wealth, the foremost wish of many Spanish from the lower nobility or hidalguía; the battle-hardened nobility that had been at war against the Muslims for eight centuries. Their soldierly merits were glorified by the famous cavalry novels of that time, and before them was a magical world full of mystery.

The younger sons of Spanish noble families, with no right to paternal inheritance and who rejected a career in the church, found in America the perfect place to accomplish military feats. These younger sons normally took the role of officers on the expeditions.

With regard to the common infantryman, their rank depended on the years of service or if he could obtain a fine sword, armour, a helmet or a good shield.

Both officers and troops were hardened men, able to traverse near-impenetrable jungles, climb snow-covered mountains or cross the scorching deserts.

They were the finest soldiers in Europe, victors over both the Moors and Christians.

Traditionally, the conquistadores have been represented as gold hungry animals, capable of the most despicable acts, but not all were cast in that mold. At that time, nobody questioned the right of conquest, not even the Aztecs. The conquistadores were indeed ambitious men, deeply imbued with the catholic faith, who took up their swords for the glory of God and their king. They sought to achieve eternal glory that would allow then into the pantheon of heroes.

◄ *THE CONQUISTADORES AT AXAYACATL'S PALACE, THEIR RESIDENCE IN TENOCHTITLAN*
Here can be seen a harquebusier wearing a bandoleer of the 'Twelve Apostles', his head covered with a morion helmet and wearing native Indian sandals. Hernán Cortés sports a cuirass and high, leather, riding boots. To his right is a sword-and-buckler man with a round shield (rodela) and wearing three-quarter length armour and burgonet, and a Spanish cavalryman wearing light armour.

CORTÉS AS SEEN BY RIVERA

In this mural by the Mexican artist Diego Rivera, Cortés is shown on the left painted as an ugly hunchback.

HERNÁN CORTÉS

Cortés himself has been universally despised, especially in Mexico where there exists not even a street, square or monument carrying his name. The famous Mexican muralist, Diego Rivera, represents Cortés in one of his historical murals as a disfigured, hunchbacked monster. Although it is true that the conquest of America caused a trauma of gigantic proportions that halted the development of a civilization, this has sadly been a universal practice. For example, the Incas erased all trace of the conquered culture to impose their own as the origin of a new civilization, before which only barbarism had existed.

In the light of world history, Cortés cannot be attributed the title of a bloodthirsty conqueror. He only resorted to the brutal, devastating violence when the circumstances did not allow him to do otherwise. He was on the verge of taking control of the Mexica Empire with minimum bloodshed, but that was no more than an illusion. How do you defeat a warlike, proud nation, as was the Mexica, without totally destroying its morale and the will of its people?

THE CONTROVERSY

Even during his lifetime he was the object of much controversy. In the crusade favouring the Indians, led by the previously mentioned friar Bartolomé de las Casas, Hernán Cortés is depicted as a cruel, bloodthirsty chieftain, whom the friar compared with the morally corrupt Nero. The destruction of Tenochtitlan, required for the success of the conquest, is compared by de las Casas with the burning of

Rome by the megalomaniac emperor. On the other hand, the Franciscan friar, Toribio de Benavente, known by the Indians as Motolinía 'the poor man', author of a story about the Indians of Nueva España and a loyal defender of the Christian conversion of the Indians, thought highly of Cortés.

'... he had faith and was a good Christian and had a very great desire to dedicate his life and possessions in order to transmit the legacy of Jesus Christ and to die for the conversion of these indigenous peoples. He spoke from his soul as the chosen one that God had put on earth as a singular captain of this western land.'

What cannot be denied is that Cortés was conscious of his destiny, which was equal to that of his opponent, the emperor Moctezuma. However, whereas the unfortunate Aztec emperor was forced by religious fatalism into depression and resignation, the Christian conqueror was endowed with an unquestioning, bold and imprudent faith. This arrogant confidence in his divine mission guided him with a firm hand, impervious to discouragement, to the destruction of an empire with a limited number of adventurers.

His Childhood

Hernán Cortés was born in the small town of Medellín in Extremadura in 1485, into a noble family of limited economic resources. His father, Martín Cortés, decided to send him, at age fourteen, to the university of Salamanca to study law. The restless boy spent two years in the classrooms in Salamanca where he learnt to write good prose and speak in fractured Latin. Books, though, were not for him. After spending a few years in the paternal household, idling and having affairs, he decided to try his luck in the Indies. In 1504, at the age of nineteen, he boarded a ship in Seville. This was the same year Queen Isabella died.

On his arrival in Hispaniola, the governor, Nicholas de Ovando, advised him to start running an 'encomienda'. *'But I have come for gold, not to work the land like a farmer'*, retorted Cortés. Despite his impatience, he spent some time in Hispaniola as an agent and notary of an establishment, until he could enlist in the expedition to Cuba led by Diego Velázquez.

Cortés in Cuba

After taking part in the conquest of Cuba, Cortés became secretary to the new governor, Velázquez. The young, frank and happy-go-lucky Extremaduran was popular among his comrades and the Spanish women. It appears that his continuous womanising resulted in him proposing marriage to a young lady, Catalina Suárez, Velázquez's sister-in-law.

The thought of marriage did not appeal to Cortés and he was unwilling to fulfil his pledge. This resulted in a reprimand by his patron, which caused Cortés to switch sides and join the people who were discontented with the Velázquez's governorship. He was bold

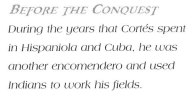

Before the Conquest

During the years that Cortés spent in Hispaniola and Cuba, he was another encomendero and used Indians to work his fields.

HERNAN CORES

to the point of proposing that he set out in a boat to Hispaniola to report what he and his companions considered abuses by the governor. Before doing so, he was captured and jailed but he escaped from captivity thus earning even greater enmity with the governor. Finally, Cortés agreed to marry Catalina Suárez and, somehow, regained the support of his new brother-in-law.

Married life made him settle down and he received a vast encomienda, with a generous number of Indians, on the outskirts of Santiago de Cuba, where he later became mayor. Within a few years, he had accumulated a sizeable fortune for the time, two or three thousand Castilians. (Medieval gold coin used in the Spanish kingdom of Castilia).

This was how things stood when Pedro de Alvarado arrived in Cuba with the gold and information from Grijalva. This caused a considerable upheaval among the citizens of the island, including Cortés. He immediately used all his wealth and possessions to charter an expedition, mortgaging and requesting credits from those willing to assist him. His young, affable character made him very popular on the island and this was the supposed reason why his late enemy and now brother-in-law, Velázquez, placed him in command of the fleet.

Nevertheless, idle tongues, encouraged by the determined and, perhaps, arrogant manner that seemed to overcome Cortés, poisoned the governor's thoughts, giving him to believe that Cortés would revolt and free himself from the obeisance expected of him. Because of this, the governor decided to replace him. When Cortés heard of the governor's plans, although he had still not completed his preparations, he decided to set sail that same night.

That was the first blow of boldness shown by Cortés who set off on his illegal expedition, leaving behind a resentful governor who would not take long in preparing his revenge.

CORTÉS' SHIPS

Cortés set sail from Cuba with eleven ships, of which only four were of a suitable tonnage. It must be remembered that, at that time, the number of barrels carried determined the measurement of a ship.

FRIARS

They were from a number of different monastic orders, like the Dominicans, as the one in this illustration, and the Franciscans.

SAILORS

They had to tend to the ships. Following Cortés' scuttling of the ships, the sailors joined the expedition as soldiers.

CARPENTERS

Among the carpenters, the 'Ribera's' stood out, as they were able to construct a boat anywhere, anytime.

▼

His flagship, the 'Santa María de la Concepción', could carry one hundred barrels, whereas the other three could only be loaded with between sixty and eighty.

These famous ships were similar to Columbus' caravels. Their development and perfection was essential for the discovery and conquest of America and its later colonization. By the close of the 15th century, the three types of Spanish ships mostly commonly used were caravels, naos and carracks, of minor to greater tonnage.

It is estimated that the measurements of the Santa María, the largest of Columbus' ships was: deck length, from stem to stern, seventy-nine feet, maximum beam twenty-six feet and height thirteen feet, with a draught of about six feet.

The ships could carry a great deal of cargo, which was necessary for the long pan-ocean voyages. The hull was round and it had three masts and square sails. The prow was reinforced with a forecastle, while the stern mounted an aftcastle, or quarterdeck where the helmsman and navigators were positioned. The forecastles and aftercastles were ideal for mounting small artillery pieces, mainly defensive, although during the conquest they were used to fire on the natives.

Along with the naos, Cortés also took with him nine smaller ships or brigantines, which could sail in shallow water and used sails or oars according to the sea condition and the circumstances. More highly manoeuvrable than the heavy naos, they were ideal for landing on beaches and in coves. They were fitted with two masts on which they could hoist square or lateen sails and could ship six oars on each side.

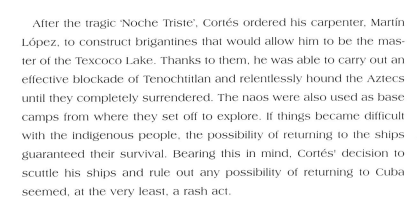

NOTARIES

Fundamental for the legal endorsement of the expedition.

SURGEONS

Necessary to tend to the many wounded.

WOMEN

Castilian women accompanied the conquest. The majority were relatives of the conquistadores.

▼

After the tragic 'Noche Triste', Cortés ordered his carpenter, Martín López, to construct brigantines that would allow him to be the master of the Texcoco Lake. Thanks to them, he was able to carry out an effective blockade of Tenochtitlan and relentlessly hound the Aztecs until they completely surrendered. The naos were also used as base camps from where they set off to explore. If things became difficult with the indigenous people, the possibility of returning to the ships guaranteed their survival. Bearing this in mind, Cortés' decision to scuttle his ships and rule out any possibility of returning to Cuba seemed, at the very least, a rash act.

THE MEMBERS OF THE EXPEDITION: THE CIVIL STAFF

Cortés took with him about five hundred and thirty Europeans. Not all of them were Spanish; among the ship's crew were about fifty Portuguese, Genoese and Neapolitans. The navigators had previously sailed with the Córdoba and Grijalva expeditions and therefore possessed knowledge of the seas and coasts they were about to encounter, which was very important on a continent that was so practically completely unknown as America. Spiritual support was also fundamental. Besides the obvious religious beliefs of Cortés and the conquistadores in general, the primary moral excuse for the conquest was to convert the Indians. For this devout work, two clergymen, friar Bartholomé de Olmedo and the Sevillian friar Juan Díaz accompanied the expedition. The latter had already accompanied Grijalva and did not know how to or did not want to get on the good

SOLDIER

Wearing armour and with a halberd, sword and Italian stockings.

▼

side of the captain. Friar Bartholomé, on the other hand, enjoyed Cortés' venture. He was a worldly, well-read man and was more interested in accompanying Cortés for the money rather than for capturing souls of the unfaithful, but he knew how to advise the captain and calm him down. There was also a doctor, Pedro López. The title of doctor may seem a little exaggerated as his functions were more that of surgeon, bloodletter and barber. There were also a dozen carpenters, who were as useful on board as they were on land, and some notaries. The function of the notaries was essential for a legal minded man like Cortés. Cortés had been appointed captain thanks to the governor who represented the crown. However, the expedition began illegally by defying the authority of Velázquez. Cortés needed to strengthen his hand legally, which is why he wrote a legal report about the movements of the campaign. Before entering into battle against the Indians he carried out the absurd procedure of reading out a request urging them to lay down their arms and declare loyalty to the Spanish emperor. Moctezuma was forced to sign documents recognising the vassalage of the King of Castile. All the establishing and founding of villages and small towns were carried out according to the rigorous bureaucratic procedure of that time. The notaries were essential for all these proceedings and more. Surprisingly, there were women present, although only comparatively few in number. One of the captains, Captain Diego de Ordas, was accompanied by his two sisters and three or four servants, and some other ladies. It is believed that they were only there to accompany their relatives and carry out domestic chores but, when necessary, they also took up arms. A few hundred Cuban Indians, who carried out the more unpleasant tasks, accompanied them along with a couple of native interpreters, Melchorejo and Francisquillo, who had been captured in Yucatan on a previous expedition.

THE SOLDIERS

The majority of the troops were Andalusian, from Seville and Huelva, a quarter were from Old Castile and the officers were mainly from Extremadura. The veterans had arrived in Hispaniola with Ovando in 1502, and had participated in the conquest of Cuba. However, many of them were young, little more than twenty years old, poor and in debt, yet bold. There were thirty crossbowmen and twelve harquebusiers. The latter were looked upon with distrust by some defenders of the medieval chivalrous ideals, but Cortés had no qualms about using the new technology. In fact, he took artillery pieces that were manned by a group of artillerymen commanded by Francisco de Orozco, veteran of the Italian wars.

The crossbowmen were under the orders of Juan Benítez and Pedro de Guzmán. The remainder of the infantry were armed according to the custom of the time and dependent on the finances of the individual soldier.

The cavalry was made up of a mere sixteen horses. While numerically few, their effectiveness was multiplied out of all proportion to their numbers as horses were unknown in the Americas and a rider could gallop through an army of Indians with the same devastating effectiveness of a scythe through a wheat field.

CORTÉS' CAPTAINS

PEDRO DE ALVARADO
(1485-1541)

Pedro de Alvarado was born in Badajoz in 1485. He arrived in the Indies in 1510 accompanied by his brothers. He participated in the conquest of Cuba and became an intimate friend of Cortés' and was one of his principal captains.

The Indians called him Tonatiuh, 'The Sun', due to his blond hair. The nickname eminently suited him because of his fiery character and the incidents of extreme cruelty that he led, including the slaughter of the cream of the Aztec aristocracy at Tenochtitlan, which ended the patience of the Aztecs and triggered 'La Noche Triste' (the Sad Night). He also participated in the conquest of Guatemala, Honduras and El Salvador and was appointed Chief Captain and Adelantado of Guatemala.

He died on the 4th of July 1541 in Nochistlan, near Guadalajara, in the area of New Galicia that is today the state of Jalisco, from injuries he sustained falling off his horse while on campaign against the Caxcanes Indians.

CRISTÓBAL DE OLID
(1487-1524)

Cristóbal, born in Zaragoza in 1487, was another one of Cortés' captains. Prototype of a conquistador, proud and rebellious, he actively participated in the conquest. Like many of his companions, he married a native woman, a tlaxaltec princess. At the siege of Tenochtitlan he had a number of confrontations with another strong character, Alvarado. These differences of opinion hindered the expedition of conquest. In 1523, following the conquest of Mexico, Cortés placed Olid in charge of the expedition for the conquest of Honduras. The impetuous Aragonese declared himself independent of the Spanish Crown and set out to conquer Honduras autonomously. He landed at Puerto Caballos and it was not long before he had all Honduras under his control. Cortés, meanwhile, sent Francisco de las Casas with two ships against him. In spite of many difficulties, Las Casas ended up capturing the rebel. Like many of his ill-fated companions, Olid came to a tragic end because of his overly excessive ambition. He was beheaded in 1524.

GONZALO DE SANDOVAL
(1497-1528)

Gonzalo was the youngest of the Conquest captains and, in many senses, the most eminent. He knew how to gain Cortés' confidence, not only because they were from the same region -Sandoval was also from Medellín- but because of the constant expressions of bravery and good judgment that the young official showed throughout the campaign. He was governor of Villa Rica in Veracruz, captured Panfilo de Narváez and, following Alvarado's disastrous slaughter in Tenochtitlan, became Cortés' first officer, the post that the violent Alvarado had previously occupied. Bernal Díaz del Castillo, the chronicler, describes him as a prudent, sensible man and a good administrator, in addition to being an excellent soldier. Sandoval often blasphemed by stating that he didn't believe in God. He accompanied Cortés, as his confidante, on his first voyage back to Spain. Soon after disembarking, he fell seriously ill and died in Palos de Moguer.

THE HORSES OF THE CONQUISTADORES

It was the conquistadores who introduced horses into America. For the indigenous people, the sight of these men mounted on such gigantic beasts was terrifying.

The riders rode with shortened stirrups, allowing them to manoeuvre with speed when reconnoitring or skirmishing. It is difficult to imagine them wearing the heavy complete armour that had already begun to lose its importance on the European battlefields. There was no necessity for it. The only recommendation that was soon revealed as fundamental in the fight against the Indians was continuous movement. Surrounded by infuriated soldiers, in the din of the battle, they were invulnerable as long as they did not stop long enough for their horses to be injured or to allow the enemy to get on the hindquarters and pull down the rider, capture him and sacrifice him before their gods.

The officers deserve a separate chapter. Cortés' situation wasn't indisputable. The captain had little or no military education except, perhaps, what he had read of battlefield tactics and strategy in Salamanca and what he had learned from the minor skirmishes against the Cuban Indians. Early in the expedition he had not had time to demonstrate his strategic abilities and some veterans watched him with gleeful satisfaction. Worse still, these veterans were in favour of governor Velázquez, and did not approve of Cortés' insubordination. Among them were prominent people such as Diego de Ordas, friend of the governor, and Francisco de Montejo, commander of one of the four naos. These, and a number of others, formed the 'Velazquista' party that caused many a headache for the Extramaduran captain, sowing discord and dividing the loyalties of the members of the expedition. Evidently, Cortés could count on his supporters and good friends, who were nearly all fellow Extremadurans. Among them was the indomitable Pedro de Alvarado and his four brothers, along with figures like Alonso Hernández de Portocarrero and the young, but efficient Gonzalo de Sandoval. Even so, the threat of the velazquistas was real and dangerous. That was the reason why the commander interpreted the role for which he seemed eminently equipped; that of a combination of charm, loquacity and flattery allied to firmness and a cruel determination. He did not hesitate to entertain any officer, even supporters of Velázquez, but neither did he hesitate to order the execution of any who conspired against him.

THE ANIMALS

It was common practice to transport live animals for their meat as well as salted and smoked meat. The chronicles report that due to Cortés' sudden departure from Cuba, he purchased all the animals he could from the island butcher in exchange for a solid gold chain. It can be

HUNTING DOGS

These animals were frequently used during the conquest of America. The harnesses and spiked collars were not only used as protection but also to increase the dog's offensive capability.

▼

taken as granted that there would be pigs, goats, sheep and possibly chickens, although these last might have been substituted by turkeys, one of the few animals that the Indians had domesticated. However, the two determinant animals in the conquest of Mexico were horses and hunting dogs. The horses impressed and frightened the indigenous people, as they had never seen them before. At first they thought they were centaurs, a confusion that led the Indians to believe that the conquistadores were Gods, *teules* in their language, sent by Quetzalcoatl to claim their kingdom. Cortés did not miss the opportunity to make the horses stamp and neigh before Moctezuma's ambassadors to fill them with both fear and admiration. Their usefulness in the war has already been commented upon. It was thanks to the cavalry, for example, that the Spaniards were able to extricate themselves from being overwhelmed at Otumba when a few riders charged through the enemy lines to the Aztec general, knocked him down and caused the confused Mexicas to withdraw.

Cortés took dogs with him; it is assumed mastiffs and wolfhounds. It was common practice to utilise them in European wars and even equip them with spiked collars and other forms of protection.

In Spain, the dogs had fought ferociously in the war against the Moors and, occasionally, the courage and fearlessness of the animal made him worthy of compensation. The Aztecs were only aware of small breeds of dogs that they bred and fattened for human consumption. These strange, fierce animals with sharp teeth, which rarely released their prey once they took hold, would only obey Gods.

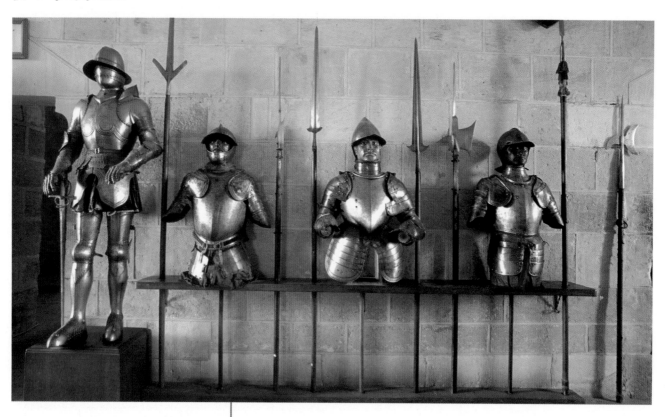

THE ARMOUR OF THE ▲
CONQUISTADORES

*Castilian Armour from the 16th
Century in the Fortress of Segovia.*

ARMAMENT

THE CAVALRY

The traditional armour of a Christian horseman of the period with all its parts can be seen in Picture 1. However, a complete set of armour was expensive, and very few could afford it. In addition, such heavy protection was unnecessary in America. Many riders preferred to replace the heavy metal breastplate with Indian *ichcaupilli*, quilted cotton vests, or with the brigandines, vests of reinforced leather with studs. Armbands, elbow pieces, cuirasses and kneepads protected arms and legs, in addition to boots and leather gloves.

The sword was the weapon par excellence. The conquistadores used both the old, heavy 15th century ones as well as the newer, lighter, streamlined ones from the 16th century. Evolution of the swords can be seen in Illustrations 2 and 3 where, over time, they also reveal how the quillons and hand guards became more sophisticated.

There were two types of shields; the adarga, an oval leather shield (Drawing 4A), inherited from the medieval Muslim armies and made of a thick piece of hardened leather, which had the advantage of being

UNEQUAL COMBAT
The natives' offensive arms were useless against an armoured knight.

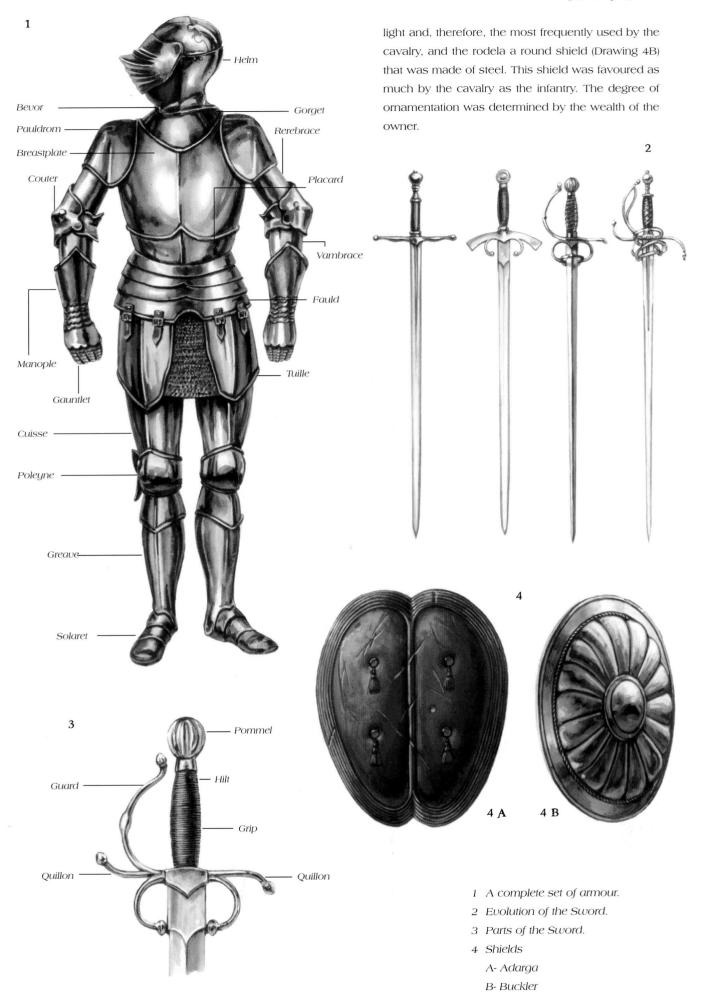

1

— Helm

Bevor —
Pauldrom —
Breastplate —

Gorget
Rerebrace

Couter —

Placard

Vambrace

Fauld

Manople

Tuille

Gauntlet

Cuisse —

Poleyne —

Greave —

Solaret —

light and, therefore, the most frequently used by the cavalry, and the rodela a round shield (Drawing 4B) that was made of steel. This shield was favoured as much by the cavalry as the infantry. The degree of ornamentation was determined by the wealth of the owner.

2

3

Pommel

Guard —

Hilt

Grip

Quillon —

Quillon

4

4 A   4 B

1 A complete set of armour.
2 Evolution of the Sword.
3 Parts of the Sword.
4 Shields
    A- Adarga
    B- Buckler

A MOUNTED SPANISH CONQUISTADOR CHARGING

Charging cavalry caused devastation among the native warriors.

▶

5

Sword-and-buckler man

The cavalry's main offensive weapon was the lance. This was lighter than the ones used by the European knights. It was used in ristre (levelled), supported on the rider's right side to take advantage of the inertia of the charge, or in 'a lanzadas' (thrust) using the strength of the arm.

THE INFANTRY

The main body of Cortés army consisted of infantrymen, organised into three groups: pike men, sword-and-shield men and crossbowmen or harquebusiers.

The infantry were protected with 'armour of three quarters', which, from what can be seen on the sword-and-shield man in Drawing 5, consisted of a helmet, gorget, breastplate and cuirass. The armour was usually painted black as a rust preventative. As with the cavalry, the veterans covered themselves with the native cotton vests while using their shields and the strength of their arm as the best protection. No matter how high the temperature, nobody removed his helmet. Apart from the closed helmet worn by the cavalry, there were four main types for the infantry (Drawing 6). The simple sallet (6A) protected the head and also had a neck protector.

At the beginning of the 16th century, the morion appeared on the scene and quickly proved very popular among crossbowmen and harquebusiers as it protected the eyes without reducing visibility. The Italian model (6B) was fitted with a crest, whereas the Spanish version (6C) finished in a type of sharp point or hook that curved rearwards.

Simpler than the morion was the cabacete (6D) with downward curving eaves.

Finally, the burgonet (6E) that was equipped with a visor, neck protector and adjustable chinstraps.

The pike men were equipped with pikes measuring from 13 to 19 feet. To be really effective, the pike men had to form a squadron.

6   6 **A**   6 **B**   6 **C**

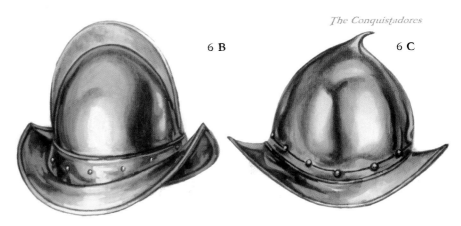

6 **D**

6 **E**

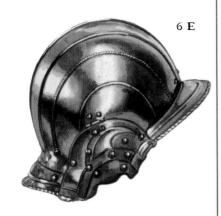

MARCHING AGAINST THE ENEMY

The conquistadores marched with their banners blowing in the wind.

The conquistadores were happier with shields and spears. They used a shorter spear, about six feet long, that was much more manageable than the pike.

THE CROSSBOW

The crossbow was a weapon that required less skill or strength than the bow. After loading, it could be calmly aimed without having to maintain the tension. As can be seen in Drawing 7, it was constructed from a number of separate

7

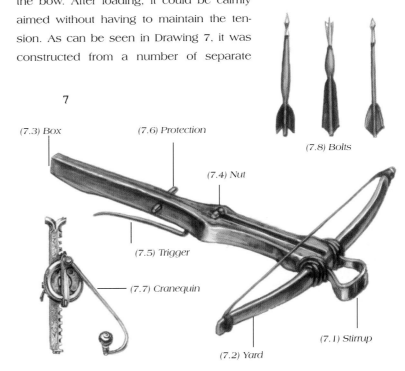

(7.3) Box   (7.6) Protection

(7.4) Nut

(7.8) Bolts

(7.5) Trigger

(7.7) Cranequin

(7.1) Stirrup

(7.2) Yard

parts. The stirrup (1), into which the foot was placed, allowed tension to be applied during the loading sequence. The arc, or yard (2) could be made from wood or metal. The box or gun carriage (3) was also made of wood and measured between two feet to three feet. The nut (4) was a small round piece of metal with projections that held the cord to maintain tension. The trigger (5) and the projection on the box (6) that

6. Helmets   6D Cabacete,

     6A Sallet,   6E Bourgonet

     6B Italian Morion,

     6C Spanish Morion,   7. Crossbow.

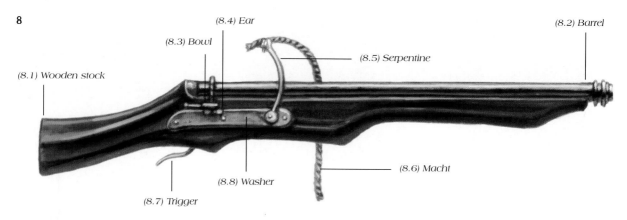

8 (8.4) *Ear*   (8.2) *Barrel*

(8.3) *Bowl*   (8.5) *Serpentine*

(8.1) *Wooden stock*

(8.8) *Washer*   (8.6) *Macht*

(8.7) *Trigger*

8. *Harquebus*

allowed the loading mechanism, or cranequin to be locked (7) were necessary to allow the cord to be tensioned. The projectiles used in combat were called bolts (8).

THE HARQUEBUS

In Drawing 8 can be seen a harquebus from the beginning of the 16th century. The parts are as follows: the wooden stock (1) and the barrel (2). During that period, a standard calibre had not been established, so that each harquebusier was forced to melt the lead and mould the balls to fit the bore of his particular weapon. The bowl (3), where a small amount of gunpowder was deposited that, when lit allowed a flame to enter a small hole, the ear (4), and ignite the gunpowder behind the ball. The serpentine (5) was a metal hook fixed to the side of the stock into which a slow match (6) was fixed. Pulling the trigger (7) released the serpentine, the slow match touched and ignited the powder in the bowl, and the shot was fired. The metal washer (8) gave cohesion to the metal joint. As with all muzzle-loading guns, the powder and ball was inserted down the barrel from the muzzle and then tamped down with the ramrod.

The harquebusiers differed from the rest of the troops and they had their own officers. In addition to the harquebus itself, they had to carry all the necessary equipment, or 'recado, to operate the guns and cannons. They wore a leather cross belt onto which was attached 'the Twelve Apostles' (Drawing 9). These were containers that contained the exact amount of gunpowder for each shot. On the same belt was carried a bag of balls, spare slow matches and two more containers, one for the gunpowder to go down the barrel and the other a finer powder, called 'prime', that, as the name suggests, was used to fill the bowl and the ear.

The harquebus ball was only effective at a distance of around fifty meters or less. In order to maintain the required rate of fire, it was necessary to organize harquebusiers so that some fired while the others loaded and so on. Contrary to what has at times been written, these firearms did not determine the outcome of any battle during the conquest. They were used more for intimidation than anything else, as the Indians had never seen anything like them.

THE ARTILLERY

When Cortés sailed from Cuba and headed for Mexico, he possessed fourteen artillery pieces, probably ten culverins and four falconets, in addition to a number of breech loading cannons called 'bombards'.

Apart from the terror that these weapons may have generated among the Indians, mouths spitting out thunder and lightning, the artillery

9

9. *Bandolier complete with 'The Twelve apostles'.*

10. Bombard

11. Culverin

12. Falconet

10

10

11

12

wreaked havoc among the Mexican infantrymen. The cannons played an important role in the final destructive siege of Tenochtitlan. Installed on board the brigantines or in locations ashore, the Spanish artillery did not stop the bombardment of the ill-fated Aztecs. The 'bombard' originated from the Middle Ages and was employed to breach the enemy walls, in some cases causing great destruction. The ones Cortés possessed were quite modest, similar to the one in Drawing 10. The bombard consisted of a thick bronze tube, 'the stock' held firmly onto a wooden frame by means of cords and iron bands. It was mounted on wheels for easy transport.

The stock was open at both ends, 'the mouth' where the bullet was emitted and, at the other end, where this and the gunpowder were introduced. Once this was done, the latter end was sealed with another metal cylinder called a 'server', and tightly fixed with a wooden wedge. The bombard was thus a breechloader.

The culverins, (Picture 11) were lighter and, therefore, more useful to Cortés. Unlike the bombards, they were muzzle-loaders, the same as the harquebuses. Culverins were much safer than the earlier breech-loaders with their 'servers'; the breech-loaders were always prone to backfiring, resulting in the death of the artillery-men. Culverins, together with bombards, were called 'thick shots'.

Another breech-loader, although much lighter than the 'thick shots, were the falconets (Drawing 12). Falconets fired balls of around six cm diameter, making them much more useful for firing against enemy troops rather than fortress walls. They were also simple to install on quarterdecks and aftercastles of the ships and brigantines, as they were small and light.

THE CONQUEST

After setting sail from Santiago de Cuba, the expedition sailed along the south of the island, arriving at Trinidad and Havana. Cortés disembarked in both ports and unfolded his banners in an attempt to encourage the Spaniards based there to join the expedition and also to obtain more equipment and provisions.

Before crossing to the continent, the charismatic commander gave a rousing speech to his men, an art in which he was a master. *'I offer you a glorious prize, but it will be only obtained through constant toil. Great things are only obtained from great efforts and glory has never rewarded the idle. If I have worked hard and gambled all my possessions on this venture, it is for the love of reputation that constitutes the noblest reward for man.*

We are few in number, but strong in courage and if this is not enough, never doubt that the Almighty, who has never abandoned the Spanish in their fight against the unfaithful, will protect you even when surrounded by a cloud of enemies, because your cause is a just cause and you are going to fight under the banner of the Cross. Let us advance then.'

ARRIVAL AT COZUMEL

After leaving Cuba on the 18th of February 1519, the expedition arrived at the island of Cozumel, on the coast of Yucatan. While here, Cortés made a valuable acquisition. As they were about to set sail, a native canoe approached the ships. On board was the unlucky Jerónimo de Aguilar who had survived a shipwreck and then spent eight years with the Indians. Aguilar was born in Écija (Seville) and had, unlike his colleagues, miraculously managed to escape sacrifice.

During his exile, Jerónimo had learned Mayan, which made him into the interpreter as Melchorejo, the Indian brought from Cuba for that function, deserted at the first opportunity.

◀ *LIFE IN THE CAMP*
God's assistance was essential for the Spaniards because, thanks to Him, the conquest was legitimized. Mass was celebrated in the conquistadores camp each day.

THE ROUTE OF THE CONQUISTADORES

Cortés' expedition from Cuba to the continent, (1518-1519)

▼

THE FIRST CONTACT

After skirting the Yucatan peninsula, the Spaniards arrived at the mouth of the Grijalva River, near the Indian town of Tabasco. Here, they received a hostile reception and Cortés had his first opportunity to demonstrate his abilities as a captain of war.

In the battle that followed, the cavalry was decisive, giving the Spaniards a magnificent victory and the submission of the Tabasquian chief. Included in the surrendered loot were twenty maidens, one of them named Malinalli, later known as Marina.

Cortés soon discovered that Malinalli spoke Mayan yucateco, the language that Aguilar was fluent in, and also *Nahuatl*, the language of the Mexicas.

Through these two interpreters, Cortés was able to converse with Teuhtlile, the first of Moctezuma's subjects that he had met.

The meeting took place on the coast, where Veracruz was later founded. The Spanish leader was eager to make contact with the lord of Mexico and introduced himself as the subject of a great emperor from overseas. Teuhtlile was astounded by the boldness of the Spaniard who had just disembarked and wanted to be received by the emperor. Despite this, he was willing to inform Moctezuma of Cortés' desire to meet him. Teuhtlile had arrived accompanied by painters who carefully drew all the details of the Spanish camp. Cortés took advantage of this to show off his cavalry and artillery to the astonished envoys.

When the great emperor Moctezuma was informed in Tenochtitlan of the arrival of the Spaniards, he called his advisors to decide what steps to take. Moctezuma was scared. Lately, the signs foretelling the arrival of misfortune had multiplied. Lake Texcoco had inexplicably risen, flooding the city. Comets, which were ill-fated omens for the Aztecs, had been seen in the sky. *Tlatoani* had nightmares; he was extremely confused and consulted with the king of Texcoco, astrologer and necromancer, who interpreted the emperor's dreams as an evident sign of the end of his reign. Some advisors were in favour of wiping out the foreigners and sending them back to sea.

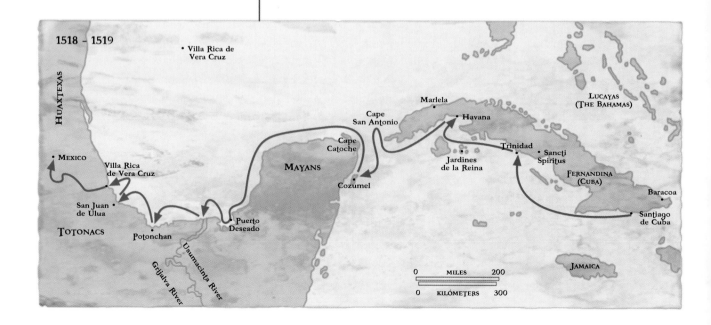

VERACRUZ

Construction of Villa Rica de Vera Cruz with the aid of the Totonac Indians.

In the end, the confused Moctezuma took the wrong decision. He sent a group of ambassadors with gifts of gold and silver to impress the foreigners while, simultaneously forbidding them to approach the capital.

If there was any doubt in Cortés' mind about the hidden wealth of the kingdom, this vanished when he saw the treasures brought by Teuhtlile on his return from Tenochtitlan. Included in the treasures were the famous Mexica calendars, which were *'as big as cartwheels'* and beautifully made in gold and silver.

Such immense wealth engendered contradictory feelings among the Spaniards. Some wanted to march without delay towards the interior, while the less courageous, primarily the Velazquistas, felt that their forces were insufficient to conquer such a fabulous kingdom. They favoured a return to Cuba to inform governor Velázquez and then return with a more powerful army.

THE DISAGREEMENT IN THE SPANISH ENCAMPMENT

A number of Indian ambassadors from the chief of the nearby city of Cempoala visited the Spanish encampment. Cempoala was the capital of the Totonaca people, which had recently been conquered by the Aztecs. The Totonacs expressed their displeasure of the Aztec repression and appealed to the foreigners for help to free them from the oppression of Tenochtitlan.

This news excited the astute Extremaduran. Until that moment, he was unaware of the internal divisions that threatened the Aztec

RUINS

Archaeological site at the Totonac city of Cempoala.

empire. Prior to this, he had been willing to conquer it by physical force but with this information everything appeared simpler. In fact, the hatred displayed by the Mexica Empire's subjects against the arrogant Aztecs, was one of the opportunities that Cortés knew how to play in his favour. However, before doing anything, he had to pacify his own troops that were threatened by the possible rift caused by the velazquistas. His cunning character was illustrated never more clearly than with the ruse he now used.

He announced publicly his desire to return to Cuba, which unleashed the wrath of those in favour of continuing with the expedition. Cortés submissively declared that, given the situation, it would be best to establish a colony in the name of the Spanish sovereigns and be able to name those who would govern it.

One of the supporters of governor Velázquez and his good friend, Alonso de Portocarrero, were chosen as mayors. Once the other aldermen and bailiffs were appointed to new Villa Rica de Vera Cruz, Cortés appeared before them, hat in his hand, and laid his position of commander at the disposal of the new council.

The newly formed council didn't take long to appoint him, in the name of the Catholic king, to the position of Commander in Chief and Greater Justice of the colony. With the stroke of a pen, Cortés had freed himself of governor Velázquez and now acted directly under royal authority and, in addition, he had made the colony's new regents accomplices of his possible irregularities. This skilful manoeuvre quietened his opponents for the moment. However, in spite of all these scheming legalities, his position remained precarious, as he could not count on the approval or confirmation of his actions on behalf of the Crown of Castile. He felt it was time to send a boat to Spain with some of the treasure. To do so, he had to ask his men to resign part of their booty, as the stipulated fifth real was not, he felt,

enough to convince the king of the treasures to come. The ship left for Spain on the 26th of July, loaded with treasures and the good wishes of the community of Villa Rica de Veracruz.

VISIT TO CEMPOALA

Once he had calmed the Spanish camp, Cortés decided to visit the chief of Cempoala in person.

This Totonaca city was the first worthy of the title that the Spaniards had seen in the New World. The chronicles report that it possessed twenty to thirty thousand inhabitants. This may appear an exaggeration, although all other testimonies from the period confirm that Nueva España was a densely populated territory and that it was the epidemics imported from Europe that provoked the catastrophic depopulation.

Cortés and his men were well received by the Cempoala chief who agreed to declare himself a subject of the King of Castile, without, surely, really being aware of what it meant. Everything went well until the *Calpixque* appeared in the city to collect Moctezuma's tax. The chief of Cempoala was scared because the Aztec civil servants reprimanded him for the welcome he had extended to the Spaniards. Cortés, the ever attentive, took advantage of the situation. He convinced the chief to arrest the civil servants. Cortés then facilitated their escape and entrusted them to tell Moctezuma that he had no wish to cause them any harm.

The audacious scheme worked and, although Moctezuma was initially irritated by the audacity of the Totonacs, he decided to pardon them when the *Calpixque*, released by Cortés, arrived at Tenochtitlan. Following this, the popularity/influence of the Spaniards in Cempoala grew enormously. They had defied *Tlatoani* and survived unharmed.

Moctezuma, meanwhile, continued to be nervous and confused. The Spaniards did not hide their intention to advance on Tenochtitlan, and he did not know how to prevent it. For the moment, he kept his eye on the situation observing, through his spies, the movements of the *teules* (foreigners).

CORTÉS SCUTTLES THE SHIPS

On Cortés' return from Cempoala to Veracruz, he found that the priest, Juan Díaz, had revived the Velazquistas conspiracy and intended to return to Cuba and inform Velázquez of what was happening.

The commander did not hesitate; he hung the conspirators, except the priest, who was saved because of his clerical condition. However, this incident pushed him into making a bold decision. Conscious that he could not allow the seed of discord to cause a split in his small army, he decided to scuttle the fleet to prevent any possibility of returning to Cuba.

The troops did not accept this daring decision at all well and they could be heard shouting around the Spanish camp *'He wants to lead us like cattle to the slaughter house'.*

The cold and calculating Cortés once again confronted his men. He, who had lost more than anyone, was the main investor of the expedi-

ENCOUNTER WITH THE ENEMY
Cortés receives the ambassadors of Moctezuma at Veracruz. In the background, the scuttled ships can be seen sinking.

tion. What use was the fleet now that they had to go inland? If they conquered, more boats would arrive. However, if they failed, they would be too far inland for the ships to be of any use. In addition, by releasing the ship's crew of the care of the naos, they could count on extra troops for the coming battle.

'As for me,' he concluded, 'I will remain here all the while at least one person accompanies me. Those cowards, who do not wish to share the dangers of our glorious challenge, go in the name of God. There is one ship left, take it and return to Cuba. There, you will be able to tell them how you deserted your commander and his companions and wait until we return loaded with the loot of the Aztecs.' A single shout rose from the camp 'To Mexico, to Mexico.'

EN ROUTE TO TENOCHTITLAN

The force that departed for the Mexican capital on the 16th of August 1519 consisted of four hundred Spaniards on foot, fifteen cavalry and seven pieces of artillery. There was also one thousand three hundred Totonac warriors and all supported by a thousand 'tamanes' or porters. A small contingent of troops remained at Villa Rica de Veracruz under the command of the bailiff, Juan de Escalante.

Little by little, the column left behind the flat coastal plain and headed into the mountains and ascended the Mexican central plateau. A few days into the trek, they arrived at the city of Tlataulitepec, where they were given a warm welcome.

Cortés, with his customary zeal, and not very diplomatically, wished to immediately convert the Indians. He had already forced the Totonacs of Cempoala to smash their idols and take up the Cross. Cortés wanted to repeat this in the new city, but the prudent intervention of father Olmedo saved the Spaniards. The priest explained that to force the indigenous people to accept the Cross was to assure that they would humiliate him as soon as his back was turned. He asked the commander to contain his religious zeal and wait for a more propitious moment. Cortés agreed. The faultless reasoning of the father prevailed over the intolerant passion of the military man.

It was necessary to continue the journey and, after seeking advice from his Indian friends, Cortés decided to go through Tlaxcala, a small country that, despite being situated at the doors of the empire, remained fiercely independent. The Spaniard thought that it would be of benefit to have them as friends, so he sent an ambassador ahead and headed for the Tlaxcaltec country.

TLAXCALA

The ambassadors that were sent to Tlaxcala did not return. Still, Cortés continued his advance until confronted by a colossal stone wall surrounding the territory. They crossed it and entered the land of Tlaxcala.

◀ *SCUTTLING THE SHIPS*
With the destruction of the ships, returning to Cuba was impossible. For Cortés and his men, their only hope was to succeed with their mission.

The Tlaxcaltecs belonged to the same family as the Mexicas and, like them, had reached the plateau towards the end of the 12th century. The country was divided into four provinces, each one governed independently by a chief. A board on which the four primary chiefs were represented, heads of the four provinces, solved any governmental matters that concerned all of them. Like the Aztecs, the society was oriented towards war, reserving the maximum honours to those citizens who distinguished themselves in the military arts. The Mexicas of Tenochtitlan had demanded the submission of Tlaxcala and had been met with ferocious resistance. Tlaxcala preferred to die before paying tribute to any foreign power. From then on, confrontations between the two countries were continuous. Mexico ordered a commercial blockade, forcing the Tlaxcaltecs to survive on their own resources, without cotton, cocoa or salt.

The children of Tlaxcala were taught from a young age to hate the Mexicans. When the Spaniards arrived the four chiefs held a meeting. On one side were those in favour of welcoming them, as they were the foreigners from the sea as foreseen by the oracle. They were the envoys of Quetzalcoatl. Others, notwithstanding, said that they could be allies of Moctezuma as they had travelled unhindered towards Tenochtitlan without any apparent opposition on the part of *Tlatoani* Mexica. Finally, ignoring Cortés' ambassadors of peace, they decided to prove the mettle of the bearded Gods. One of the chiefs, Xicoténcatl the Old, was in favour of attacking the Spaniards and proposed that the army, led by his son, the brave young Xicoténcatl, fought them without delay.

▶

THE COUNCIL OF TLAXCALA
The meeting of the four chiefs of the four provinces forming the state. This council initially decided to attack the Spaniards, thinking that they were, perhaps, allies of Moctezuma, their mortal enemy.

guzmā. mchvacā.

Allies

The Tlaxcaltecs fight alongside the Spaniards. The banner with its illustration of the heron on the back of a soldier was the emblem of the house of Xicoténcatl, the great Tlaxcaltec leader.

Cortés faced the fierceness of the Tlaxaltecs in a couple of confrontations and only survived the encounters thanks to the opportune intervention of the artillery. Indeed, the Spaniards never faced such audacious and disciplined soldiers in America, as the Tlaxaltecs maintained the formation of their lines even while they retreated.

If the Tlaxaltecs were like this, what would the feared Mexicas be like?

Cortés continued sending peace ambassadors to the capital. Eventually they returned with the message that the young Xicoténcatl, with an army of five battalions, each of ten thousand men, was ready to annihilate the foreigners.

On the morning of the 5th of September 1519, Cortés reviewed his troops. With their stomachs tight with fear but their hearts overflowing with courage, they listened to the words of their commander. '*If we fail now*', he said, '*the Cross of Christ will never be planted in this land! Go forward my companions! When has it ever been that a Castilian turned his back on the enemy?*'

Before them, never ending lines of the enemy stretched across the horizon headed by a banner of the white heron, the symbol of the house of Xicoténcatl.

As soon as the Castilians appeared, the air vibrated with the deafening shouts of the Tlaxcaltecs, the beating of drums and the blowing of large shells. The sky darkened with the rain of arrows and darts

DIPLOMACY AND VIOLENCE
Hernán Cortés knew how to combine diplomatic flattery with devastating violence. Allies were treated with respect, while enemies were shown no mercy.

falling on that small group of Spaniards who, seeing a tidal wave of infuriated natives advancing on them, had the fortitude to hold the formation and to fire their harquebusiers.

Time and time again, Xicoténcatl sent his troops down onto that armoured rock that, although it shook and hesitated, resisted the fury of the Tlaxcaltec. Toledo's steel blades tore through their ranks, ruthless and cold in a constant slaughter, without rest. The horses charged, retreated and charged again. But the Tlaxaltecs were not able to take advantage of their overwhelming numerical superiority. Although they were distributed across different independent companies, they moved in a confused mass, badly directed and crowding together in their eagerness to get at the Spaniards. The young Xicoténcatl did not know how to concentrate his forces, although he maintained a constant pressure by using part of his troops consecutively, relieving and supporting each other, only a small portion of that immense army was able to make contact with the enemy, which was so few in number, at any one time. Meanwhile, the rest of the army remained inactive at the rear, uselessly pressing forward and impeding the movements of their companions.

If they had kept up a continuous attack on the Spaniards, relieving each other in an orderly fashion, Cortés and his four hundred men would have had to surrender from sheer exhaustion. Christian Providence helped the crusader by causing widespread discord among the Tlaxcaltecs troops. One chief decided to withdraw his troops due to an argument with Xicoténcatl. Finally, witnessing the incompetence of his troops, Xicoténcatl withdrew, leaving the Spanish masters of the field, wounded and at breaking point, but victorious. The victory was decisive. While the Spanish still had to repulse further attacks and conspiracies from the proud Xicoténcatl, he finally agreed to follow the orders of the Tlaxcaltec board and accept his defeat. From that moment, Tlaxcala became one of Cortés' firmest allies in his confrontation with Tenochtitlan.

Moctezuma had hoped that the Spaniards would have met their maker in Tlaxcala. Not only had this not happened, but also the contenders had become Cortés' allies against him. He saw Cortés as the one revealed by the omens, the hand destined to snatch away his throne. He sent a new ambassador to the Spaniards, loaded with treasures and pleaded for them not to enter his capital. He was prepared to do whatever had to be done to avoid meeting them.

Moctezuma showed his weaknesses at the same time as the ambassadors from all over Mexico arrived at the Tlaxcaltec palace, where Cortés had installed himself, to pay their respects. One of them was Ixtlilxochitl, prince of Texcoco, who hated Moctezuma and came to offer Cortés his services against the detested *Tlatoani*.

THE MASSACRE AT CHOLULA

While they were still in Tlaxcala, a new ambassador arrived from Moctezuma inviting them to visit Tenochtitlan. He recommended that they take the Cholula route, a friendly town where they would be guests of honour. Cortés' new Tlaxcaltecs allies warned him of the duplicity of the *Tlatoani* and his wicked intentions. Aware that they could be walking into a trap, the Spanish army left Tlaxcala and resumed their march on Mexico taking the Cholula route. Six thousand Tlaxcaltecs warriors, who were valuable allies, accompanied them.

Cholula was, at the time of the conquest, one of the most prosperous and populated cities in the Anahuac valley. It was an old city, founded by the races that inhabited the plateau before the arrival of the people of *Nahuatl* speech, like the Mexicas. Cholula was the main commercial centre of the Mexica Empire and also an important religious capital. Tradition associated it with Quetzalcoatl and its huge number of pyramids and temples turned it into something like the Mecca of the Mexican religion. It was the holy city of the Anahuac.

DESTRUCTION OF THE ENEMY
With their new allies, the Tlaxcaltecs, the Spaniards carried out the massacre in the city of Cholula, the Tenochtitlan ally.

THE MARK OF THE CONQUEST

Ruins of an old Tlaxcaltec pyramid.

▼

The Spaniards were well received by the Cholultecs who only asked that the Tlaxaltec contingent, traditional enemies of the Cholula, pitch camp on the outskirts of the town.

However, the friendly reception was no more than the bait for the trap. In a desperate attempt to change their destiny, the Aztec priests had told their emperor that the omens were favourable and that everything indicated that the Spaniards could be destroyed in the holy city of Cholula. The gods would surely not abandon them in the sacred city.

Thanks to the intervention of Marina, the plot was uncovered. A Cholultec noble had warned the interpreter of what was about to occur and invited her to flee from her evil masters. It would appear that Marina had either already been seduced by Cortés, or the Spaniards or, perhaps, also detested the Aztecs. Whatever the case, she informed her lover and captain, who did not take long to warn his men and take the necessary steps.

They first announced their departure for Tenochtitlan. On the appointed morning, the whole of the Spanish army lined up in the main square of Cholula, blocking and guarding all the entrances. The leading residents of Cholula went to the square to bid farewell to those they imagined would soon be victims. But their perceived good fortune had turned. Cortés gave the order, the square was closed preventing anyone from fleeing or others gaining access to come to their aid, and the killing began. This soon became a massacre when the Spaniards allowed the Tlaxcaltecs, who were quartered outside the city, to enter and the city became a welter of blood and fire. It was a terrible slaughter that deeply shocked all the inhabitants of Mexico. The white Gods were invincible and their fury was terrifying.

*NUESTRA SEÑORA
DE LOS REMEDIOS*

The church of Nuestra Señora de
los Remedios was built on the
ruins of the Great Pyramid of the
Sun of Cholula.

*THE ROUTE
TO TENOCHTITLAN*

The route taken by the Spaniards
from the coast to the Mexica
capital.

Disturbed by the failure of his plans, Moctezuma sent a new ambassador to Cortés in which he dissociated himself from the Cholultec betrayal. Cortés pretended to believe him and told the ambassadors that he would soon depart bound for the Mexica capital. Before leaving Cholula, Cortés wanted to convert the city but, once again, the intervention of father Olmedo convinced him that it was hopeless to attempt to Christianize a town that had, until the previous day, been the main religious sanctuary of Mexico. Cortés agreed, but no one could prevent him from placing an immense Cross on the top of the Cholula's largest temple.

After a three-day march, the Spaniards looked over the wonder of the valley where Lake Texcoco shone in the sunlight and the beauty of it all touched their hearts. It was a fertile valley, full of towns and villages of shining white houses, of cultivated fields, leafy forests and aromatic gardens. The vibrancy of a great civilization beat all around them.

As they marched, they were met by crowds of indigenous people curious to see the *teules*. Nevertheless, there was no display of hostility.

Moctezuma remained locked in his palace, subject to terrible fasting and looking for relief in the prayers of the gods. 'What good is it to resist if the Gods are against us?'

The astonished Spaniards arrived on the shores of Lake Chalco and set foot on one of the roads, firmly set on the lakebed, which led to Tenochtitlan, the American Venice. They crossed Lake Chalco and, before continuing on the road that crossed Lake Texcoco, they stayed in the city of Iztapalapa, famous for its heavenly gardens that were tended with great care and delicacy by the lord of the city.

Cortés lay on a mat with Marina, drunk from the exotic tropical aromas that came from the garden, but he did not sleep. He imagined the enchanted city, Tenochtitlan, which he would enter the following morning.

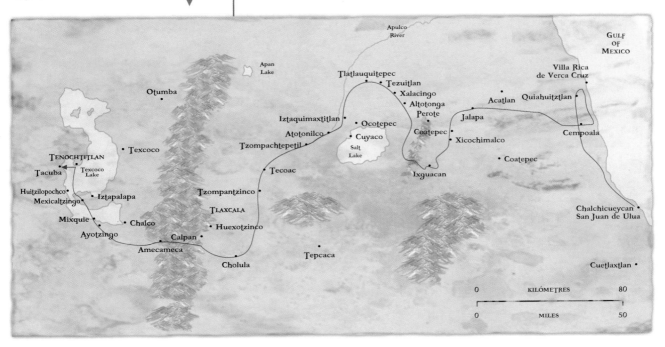

DOÑA MARINA
(1502–1529)

Malinalli was born in Coatzacoalcos into a noble family. According to legend, as a result of a family conspiracy, she was sold as a slave when she was a young girl. This ensured that she spoke two languages, Nahuatl, her mother tongue, and Mayan yucateco, her master's language. The chiefs of Tabasco gave her to Cortés as part of the war booty. Cortés' interpreter, Jerónimo de Aguilar, spoke Mayan that was why, together with the Indian girl, by now baptized Marina, they could translate the Nahuatl, language of the Mexicas, into Castilian. Cortés took her under his wing and she later became his mistress. Marina quickly learned Castilian, making her an essential figure during the conquest. Through her influence, the Aztecs named Cortés, Malintzin, pronounced Malinche: Lord of Malinalli. Over time, Marina also became known as Malinche. Despite bearing Cortés a son, at the conclusion of the conquest, Cortés married her off to another conquistador, Juan Jaramillo.

▲ Hernán Cortés and Doña Marina
Museum of America (Madrid).

◄ THE RECEPTION OF THE AMBASSADORS
Cortés used the services of Marina to parley with the Mexican lords and their ambassadors.

A GOOD BEGINNING

Following the orders of Tlatoani *Moctezuma, the Mexicas give the Spaniards a warm welcome.*

THE ENTRANCE TO TENOCHTITLAN

On the morning of the 8th of November 1519, Hernán Cortés readied himself to enter Tenochtitlan at the head of his small army. He led the column with the cavalry section, followed by the infantry, with the impedimenta (baggage train) in the centre and the fierce Tlaxcaltecs bringing up the rear. There were no more than seven thousand in total, of which only four hundred were Spanish.

They walked towards the city on the South road, flanked by myriads of canoes full of Indians who, from the lake, curiously observed the parade.

Cortés may have thought that entering a city like Tenochtitlan, in the middle of a lake, into which there was only three access roads, was stepping into a dangerous, deadly trap.

Eventually, the impressive imperial entourage stopped them on their way and Moctezuma descended from his gold palanquin and walked upon a fine cotton carpet to meet with Cortés. The Spanish commander, resplendent in his brilliant armour, dismounted to greet the powerful monarch. Through Marina, Moctezuma expressed his satisfaction at seeing the Spaniards in his capital and assigned his brother to be their host in charge of accommodating them. Cortés thanked the sovereign for his generosity who then departed with the highest respects of consideration.

For their accommodation, the Spaniards were given Moctezuma's father's palace, Axayacatl. It was so big that it could accommodate, without any problem, the Spanish Tlaxcaltec army among the buildings, courtyards and gardens.

Cortés kept up his guard and forbade his men to leave the palace, threatening them with death if they disobeyed, and he guarded it accordingly.

Moctezuma was, it appeared, willing to impress the Spaniards with his generosity and affability. The attention and gifts they received multiplied and the Spanish camp was generously supplied. It was difficult to believe that this generous monarch was the same person that had terrified the Mexicans with the mention of his name.

MEXICA ART
A ceramic Mexica statue representing a warrior from the military order of the eagle.

Cortés didn't waste time and requested to be received in the imperial palace. Moctezuma gladly accepted, and showed the Spaniards that *Tlatoani* lived in such luxury that he had no reason to envy other of the world's monarchs.

Accompanied by Father Olmedo, the Spanish commander spoke about his favourite topic, the Christianization of the Indians. It's believed that the intervention of the friar smoothed Cortés' somewhat brusque manner when he was in his evangelizing state of mind.

Obviously, Moctezuma could not abjure the faith that was the essence of himself and of his city. It was not worth the trouble to discuss it more. However, he recognized the Spaniards as the long foreseen envoys of the tradition and the oracles who had arrived to retake their kingdom.

'I know that your sovereign from beyond the seas is the legitimate owner over this kingdom which until now I have governed. So you Malinche, (the name by which he called Cortés), you can give orders because you will be obeyed and everything I have is at your disposition.'

The story should have ended here, but destiny had many more chapters to write. It was not going to be so simple.

Tlatoani's continuing generosity and willingness to recognize the sovereignty of the Spaniards gained him the respect and consideration of the coarse conquistadores. Cortés clearly did not believe that the monarch would renounce his dominion so easily or with such good grace or and that his city would allow it. For the moment, however, he decided to inspect the city.

The Captive Emperor

By virtue of their august host, the Spaniards knew the impressive Tlatelolco market. They were overwhelmed by the enormous variety of products and business dealings, both of which demonstrated that the valley of Mexico was both highly populated and prosperous.

They went to the top of the pyramid, or temple that was at the city's centre, and where Tlaloc and Huitzlipochtli were worshipped. They saw the piles of skulls and smouldering hearts that had recently been ripped out and offered to the protecting divinity. The impetuous Cortés dared to reproach *Tlatoani* about his deviant cult. This, of course, angered Moctezuma who then had to make amends with his Gods because of the insult received from his guests. The Spaniards persisted in their eventual aim, and asked permission to build a chapel in the palace where they were quartered. While cleaning and preparing to begin the construction, they discovered the treasure of king Axayacatl behind a false wall. This had been preserved after the king's death according to the Mexican tradition. In spite of the excitement caused by the immense wealth, far more than they had imagined, they had to contain their avarice until a more opportune moment. They resealed the door and remained quiet about their discovery.

They had by now been in Mexico for a week and the emperor continued overwhelming them with his generous hospitality, but... how long would it last? They were in a very precarious situation. Any small event could trigger unexpected consequences and the Spaniards would be trapped in the palace, surrounded by enemies and without a possibility of escape. Cortés was unable to tolerate the situation any longer and he proposed a daring coup to his officials, to seize Moctezuma and bring him to the Spaniards' quarters.

On the morning chosen for the dangerous undertaking, father Olmedo prayed to the saints for it to be blessed. Armed with the conviction that the saints were on their side, the small army distributed themselves strategically along the streets that went from their palace to the emperor's.

Accompanied by five of his best horsemen, Cortés requested to be received by *Tlatoani*. He politely invited the unfortunate monarch to change residence and to transfer to the Spanish quarters as a sign of goodwill and submission to the authority of the Spanish sovereign *'Even if I agreed to such degradation, my subjects never would.'* The irate Moctezuma exclaimed.

Only the threat of death made him reconsider his decision and he finally acceded to the Spaniard's request. Crestfallen, he looked to have all his courtly pomp around in the pretence that his move was voluntary.

Cortes, Lord of Mexico

With that bold move, Hernán Cortés became the governor of Mexico using the captive sovereign as an instrument. He ordered two brigantines to be constructed, thus making his control over the lake easier. He sent detachments to different parts of the country and to even found colonies.

MOCTEZUMA'S RECEPTION

The encounter between two worlds was symbolized in the reception that the Mexica sovereign, Moctezuma, offered to the Spaniards on their arrival at Tenochtitlan.

MOCTEZUMA TAKEN CAPTIVE

Hernán Cortés decides to take Moctezuma hostage and transfer him to the Spaniards quarters in another palace.

▶

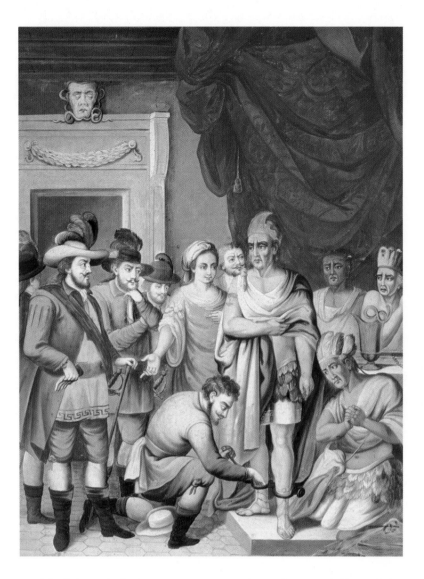

He jailed the rebel, Cacama, Moctezuma's nephew and king of the Texcoco, who wanted to start a conspiracy against the hated foreigners. Moctezuma collaborated in all of this, and more, placing all the kingdom's resources at Cortés' feet.

The moment had come to legitimize the achievements in writing. The monarch also docilely agreed to this and obliged his chieftains to officially recognize the authority of King Charles. This was done in a solemn ceremony, and an official report was made by the royal notary to send to Castile. Everything appeared under control but, once again, the commander had to resort to his incredible powers of persuasion to silence the displeasure that had risen in the Spanish troops by the perceived unjust distribution of the fabulous war booty. His offer to divide his portion with the dissatisfied men maintained the peace in the camp and allowed him to return his attention towards his great obsession.

He demanded that the Tenochtitlan temple be handed over to him so that he could consecrate it in the name of the Christian God. The horrified protests of Moctezuma and his warnings that such sacrilege would provoke a revolt among the people did not stop the fanatically religious Extremaduran.

Huitzilipochtli and Tlaloc were pulled down from their altars and replaced with the Virgin and the Cross. An air of desolation and depression descended from the peak of *Teocalli*, impregnating the town, sinking it in a tense calmness.

THE CITY OF TENOCHTITLAN

Like an American Venice, the Mexica capital rose in the middle of Lake Texcoco, complete with canals.

▼

Moctezuma now changed his attitude and requested, with cold courtesy, that the Spaniards leave the city, the sooner the better because he could not contain the anger of his people for much longer. The offended Gods demanded the blood of the foreign violators.

Cortés asked for time, as he needed to build brigantines in order to return to his mother country. Moctezuma agreed. He wanted to avoid a war between his people and the Spaniards at all costs. A war, that according to the gods they were sure to lose. He managed to contain the rage of his city by announcing the prompt departure of the Spaniards, but the cracks in his authority now grew by the minute.

The Spanish camp was practically under siege. They had entered Tenochtitlan six months earlier and, in one day, their evangelical mission had turned them from envoys from the Gods to profane, sacrilegious heretics. At the beginning of May 1520, news arrived from the coast that placed Cortés and his men in a yet more difficult situation.

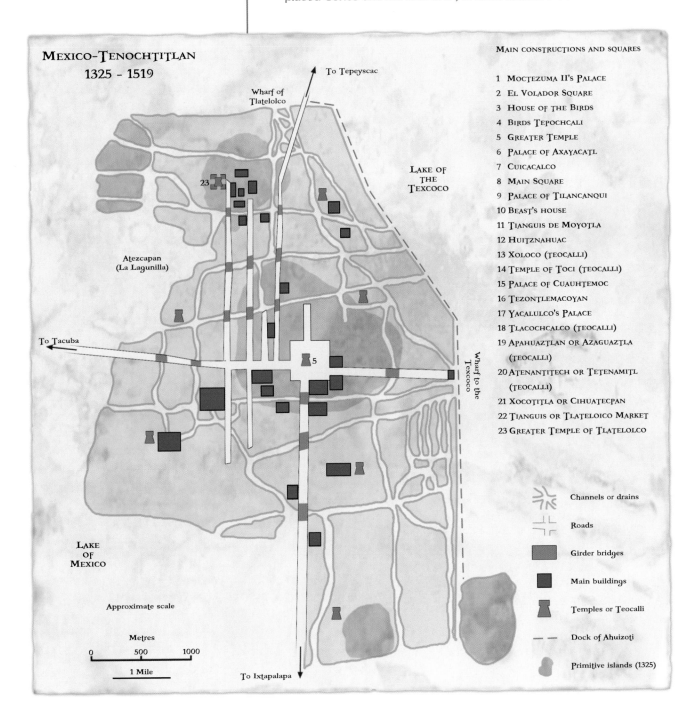

MEXICO-TENOCHTITLAN
1325 – 1519

To Tepeyscac

Wharf of Tlatelolco

LAKE OF THE TEXCOCO

Atezcapan (La Lagunilla)

To Tacuba

Wharf to the Texcoco

LAKE OF MEXICO

Approximate scale

Metres

0   500   1000

1 Mile

To Ixtapalapa

MAIN CONSTRUCTIONS AND SQUARES

1 MOCTEZUMA II's PALACE
2 EL VOLADOR SQUARE
3 HOUSE OF THE BIRDS
4 BIRDS TEPOCHCALI
5 GREATER TEMPLE
6 PALACE OF AXAYACATL
7 CUICACALCO
8 MAIN SQUARE
9 PALACE OF TILANCANQUI
10 BEAST'S HOUSE
11 TIANGUIS DE MOYOTLA
12 HUITZNAHUAC
13 XOLOCO (TEOCALLI)
14 TEMPLE OF TOCI (TEOCALLI)
15 PALACE OF CUAUHTEMOC
16 TEZONTLEMACOYAN
17 YACALULCO'S PALACE
18 TLACOCHCALCO (TEOCALLI)
19 APAHUAZTLAN OR AZAGUAZTLA (TEOCALLI)
20 ATENANTITECH OR TETENAMITL (TEOCALLI)
21 XOCOTITLA OR CIHUATECPAN
22 TIANGUIS OR TLATELOICO MARKET
23 GREATER TEMPLE OF TLATELOLCO

Channels or drains

Roads

Girder bridges

Main buildings

Temples or Teocalli

Dock of Ahuizoti

Primitive islands (1325)

▲

THE DEFEATED ENEMY

*A modern bas-relief showing
Gonzalo de Sandoval, Cortés'
favourite captain, receiving the
submission of the king of Colima
after the capitulation of
Tenochtitlan in 1521.*

GOVERNOR VELÁZQUEZ'S REVENGE

Cortés' worst fears came true when his appointed governor at Villa Rica de Veracruz informed him that a squad had arrived from Cuba, sent by governor Velázquez, under the command of Pánfilo de Narváez.

They had arrived aboard eighteen naos with nine hundred infantrymen, eighty cavalry, harquebusiers and crossbowmen, in addition to artillery and plentiful ammunition. They brought with them an arrest warrant against the Extremaduran and, with it, a claim from the Cuban governor for all that Cortés had accumulated.

Cortés' was even more decisive when faced with difficulties. He sent an ambassador to Narváez's camp with a large amount of gold booty and led by the prudent father Olmedo while, at the same time, he made military preparations. Leaving a garrison in Tenochtitlan under the command of Alvarado, he left for the coast with a contingent of seventy veterans. Along the way he met with Captain Velázquez de Leon and his one hun-

PÁNFILO DE NARVÁEZ
1470-1528

Friar Bartolomé de las Casas, who knew the conquistador well, says of him: 'He was a man of authority, tall, blonde, honest, wise but not very prudent. Of good conversation and customs and who also made an effort when fighting the Indians. However, he had one principal fault, he was very careless.'

He was friend and lieutenant of governor Velázquez and this was the reason why he was assigned to lead the mission to capture the rebellious Cortés. He was not equal to the intrepid Extremaduran who held him captive for a couple of years. On his release, Narváez was given the royal appointment of Captain for the conquest and colonization of Florida. He set sail from Spain on 17th of June 1527 with a fleet of five naos and six hundred men.

Narváez's unlucky star accompanied him on his new expedition that was little more than a litany of misfortune. Overcome by a violent storm, they were shipwrecked on the coast of American. Many of drowned, among them Captain Panfilo de Narváez. It was the year 1528.

dred and twenty men, whom he had earlier sent on a mission of exploration. Arriving at Cempoala, he met with his governor from Veracruz, the intrepid Gonzalo de Sandoval, who duly informed his captain of the condition and movements of Narváez and his men.

Shortly after, father Olmedo arrived with the information that Narváez had refused to reach an agreement and wanted to see Cortés in chains. However, Panfilo's officers thought differently. They all realized that a battle between Spaniards would ruin the course of the conquest. They deplored the vindictive obstinacy of Narváez, a mirror image of his master, the governor. Olmedo had secretly distributed the gold among Narváez's disgruntled men who then formed a Cortesian party. From here on everything was simple.

Just over two hundred of Cortés' veterans stormed Narváez's camp on a rainy night. Surprised, the novices were caught unawares or did not want to offer much resistance. Narváez lost an eye in the fray and surrendered easily. It was all over! After Cortés gave an eloquent speech full of promises of gold and wealth, backed up with stories related by the veterans, all the Spaniards formed up under the flag of the audacious conquistador.

Hernán Cortés returned to Mexico accompanied by a thousand infantry, among them harquebusiers and crossbowmen, and over one hundred cavalry. While all were well equipped, they were not as well trained as Cortés' veterans.

▶

A NEW FAITH
Friar Bartolomé de Olmedo
attempts to convert Moctezuma
and his chieftains to Christianity.

The jubilation, however, was short lived. Misfortune always comes in blocs. As they approached Tenochtitlan, news was received that the city had risen up and Alvarado and his men were cornered and required assistance.

The march quickened pace across a country that now looked upon them with hostility. On the 24th of June 1520, they once again arrived at the road across the lake. It was all so different now. A highly threatening silence surrounded them. There were no canoes on the lake and the streets were deserted. Finally, they arrived at the Axayacatl palace where they were greeted with relief by the besieged.

ALVARADO MASSACRES THE NOBLES

What had happened? The Mexicas had to mark one of the main celebrations of their religious calendar in honour of their God Huitzilipochtli. They requested permission from Alvarado to carry out their rituals in the square of the great *teocalli* and he had no problem in granting it. On the indicated day, the principal nobles of the Mexica aristocracy were brought together in the square, dressed in their finest attire. Deeply involved in the religious practice they were unable to react when Alvarado and his men burst into the celebration with swords drawn and slaughtered everyone. There were over six hundred and they all perished because the Spaniards, as in Cholula, had blocked all the entrances to the square preventing anyone from fleeing.

Why did they do it? Alvarado swore to Cortés that he had clear indications that a conspiracy was being prepared and that it was the only way to prevent it. However, many attributed the misfortune to Alvarado's violent nature. For such a delicate mission, he was the least appropriate captain to remain behind considering that the Mexicas were already angry when Cortés left the city for his encounter with Narváez.

Be as it may, the savage killings triggered off the most fierce insurrection. Once again, Moctezuma was forced to intervene to calm his people who, although interrupting the attacks, maintained the blockade. The blockade was only opened to allow Cortés and his men to enter and closing it again to trap them.

Provisions did not arrive in the Spanish camp, which was threatened by hunger. Cortés decided to release Moctezuma's brother, Cuitlahuac, who he also held captive and give him the mission to act as mediator with the insurrectionists. After gaining his freedom, Cuitlahuac claimed his right to the throne and he was chosen as the new sovereign instead of the unfortunate Moctezuma. The fierce Aztec city could not any longer tolerate the humiliating servitude of the long time powerful *Tlatoani* and decided to depose him.

The new *Huei Tlatoani* took up the direction of the army and decreed the immediate extermination of the loathsome foreigners.

◀ *THE MASSACRE*
When Cortés set off for his encounter with Narváez, he left a garrison in Tenochtitlan under the command of Pedro de Alvarado. This violent conquistador slaughtered the Mexica nobles under the pretext of a perceived coup and infuriated the Aztecs.

THE DESTRUCTION OF THE TEMPLE

Hernán Cortés and his men demolish the idols in the great temple of Tenochtitlan.

▼

THE DEATH OF MOCTEZUMA

The inhabitants of Tenochtitlan took up arms and surged forward en masse to the palace where the Spaniards were quartered and trapped.

The pent up rage, which had been restrained for so long because of Moctezuma's submissiveness, overflowed. Over the Axayacatl palace courtyard rained down arrows, stones and lances. Only the artillery and harquebusiers were able to contain the infuriated Mexicas. Because of the unexpected ferocity of the siege, Cortés decided to go out and show them the power of the lord of the capital. While he caused havoc among the Aztec troops, the enemy was without number and untiring and each loss of a Spaniard brought them closer to annihilation.

The only option left was to turn to the unfortunate Moctezuma to see if he still retained any influence in his city and calm the insurrection.

'It will not make any difference. They will not listen to me nor Malinche. You will never leave these walls alive.' responded the depressed monarch. Their threats could no longer persuade him and only when they assured him that the only thing they wanted was to be allowed to leave the capital, Moctezuma agreed.

When he appeared on the terrace of the palace dressed in his royal finery, the fighting stopped and all were quiet. However, the Mexicas had had enough of the incomprehensible meekness of this once fearsome man. When he asked for mercy for the Spaniards, the shouting and the rain of projectiles resumed. A stone struck Moctezuma on the head

knocking him down. The Spaniards covered him as quickly as possible and took him to his room.

He had been rejected by his own people, he had no reason to continue living. He refused all care and also refused to speak. Within a few days, the deep anguish he felt took him from this world. Before dying, he had the fortitude to reject the inopportune baptism that father Olmedo tried to insist he accept. With Moctezuma dead there were no more trump cards to play. The Spaniards were further agitated when it was discovered that all the bridges had been destroyed thus preventing anyone from escaping. It was now necessary to break out and somehow escape at all costs.

'LA NOCHE TRISTE'

Of the three docks or roads entering Tenochtitlan, the Spaniards chose to escape across the westerly one, leading to Tlacopan. It had the advantage of being the shortest of the routes and would allow the fugitives to reach dry land quicker than the other two. The drawback was that it had three canals that also had to be crossed and the bridges had been destroyed. Cortés ordered the speedy construction of a portable wooden bridge over which the army could pass. There was no time to lose. Night was the chosen time for the escape attempt and Cortés gave his final instructions. It was not possible to take all the gold, so the commander gave the troops permission to take what they wanted. He recommended them to be prudent, warning them that too much of a load could hinder the escape. The veterans heeded his advice, while Narváez's inexperienced conscripts ignored it and greedily filled their pockets.

The order of the march was to be, in the vanguard two hundred infantrymen under the orders of Gonzalo de Sandoval, and supported by twenty cavalrymen. Bringing up the rear, Pedro de Alvarado with the bulk of the infantry while, in the centre was to be Cortés with the baggage and treasure. The Tlaxcaltecs allies were distributed between the three divisions. On the night of the 1st July 1520, under a warm drizzle, the Spaniards stole out of the palace and crept along the dark, deserted

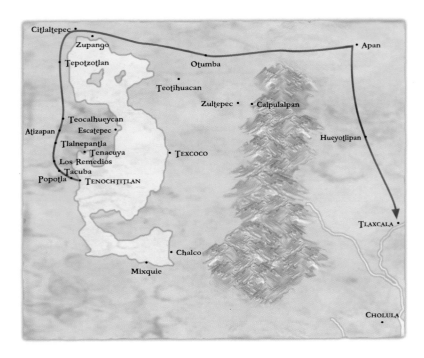

EN ROUTE TO TLAXCALA
The route taken by the Spaniards after withdrawing from Tenochtitlan to Tlaxcala following 'La Noche Triste'.

streets of the apparently sleeping city. They arrived at the road without mishap and then, on entering the road, there was an outburst of shouting accompanied by the blowing of the conch shells, all lit up by the light of numerous fires. From the dark waters of the lake could be heard the fearsome murmur of canoe paddles approaching at great speed. Again, a hailstorm of projectiles descended on them.

The improvised bridge was laid down over the first canal and crossed without hesitation. There was no time to fight back. However, the advance was slow and, by the time the vanguard reached the second canal, the rearguard had not completed the crossing of the portable bridge at the first canal. Even greater misfortune then struck, as there was no way to return to collect the bridge when all had passed over, as it had become jammed in a rock. It was now impossible to proceed and also impossible to withdraw. In the middle of the floating dock, harassed by thousands of canoes full of bloodthirsty natives, the Spaniards and Tlaxcaltecs fought with the desperation of despair. The huge losses mounted, indeed so many that the second canal, now filled with the bodies of dead horses and men, allowing the survivors to use them as an improvised bridge and continue the escape. Yet, there was still the third canal to cross. On reaching the third canal, without hesitation the soldiers dived into the water and swam to the other side. Finally, the vanguard reached firm ground, but Alvarado and his men were still trapped on the road. Cortés returned with some cavalrymen to assist the rearguard. Alvarado, meanwhile, had been knocked down but still tried, without success, to reunite his column. An overwhelming tide of enemies surrounded them. Many fell into the water, and were drowned because of the weight of their arms and gold, while many others were captured alive to be sacrificed to the Gods. Assisted by the reinforcements, the survivors ran towards the third canal that they also had to swim across. Finding himself left behind, Alvarado took hold of a pike, ran to the canal and sinking the pike into the heart of the lake, vaulted magnificently over the gap.

Once firm ground had been reached, the persecution ended. The Spaniards found shelter in which to rest and to take stock of the magnitude of their misfortune. All the treasure, artillery and gunpowder had been lost. The Spanish army had been reduced to little more than a third and their Tlaxcaltecs allies had lost more than two thousand men. The chronicles say that Cortés cried over the defeat, but his spirit was unweakened. On being informed that Marina and Martín López, the carpenter, had survived he began to plan his return.

THE BATTLE OF OTUMBA

The Mexicans did not continue to pursue the Spaniards, if they had done so they would surely have destroyed them. They also delayed the cleaning and reconstruction of the city as they celebrated their religious rituals of gratitude, offering their Gods the still-beating hearts of the detested *teules*.

This allowed the Spaniards time to compose themselves, and to seek refuge in the only place where they would be safe, the republic of Tlaxcala.

On the seventh day of the march they arrived on the plain of Otumba, where the new *Tlatoani*, Cuitlahuac, had assembled his army to once

◀

'LA NOCHE TRISTE'

The biggest defeat suffered by the Spaniards during the conquest of Mexico, was the so-called 'La Noche Triste', when they were attacked en masse by the inhabitants of Tenochtitlan while withdrawing from the city.

and for all eliminate the Spaniards. Even Cortés, on seeing the huge enemy army with its colourful banners waving in the sun, covering the ground as far as the eye could see and comparing it with his meagre army weakened by hunger and exhaustion, felt that his last hour had arrived. Confident that the God that had taken them there would not abandon them at such a critical moment, the small army, with its prickly display of swords and pikes, stayed their ground like a rock against the waves.

After several hours of unremitting combat, the Spaniards were weak with exhaustion. At that critical moment, the untiring commander spotted, between the multitudes of soldiers, the palanquin of the Mexica *Cihuacoatl*, commander of the army. The bright trimmings and colourful banners made it unmistakable. Quickly, Cortés, followed by a handful of cavalrymen, charged through the enemy troops directly at the chief, second in importance to *Tlatoani* in Aztec society. *Cihuacoatl's* personal guard were impotent against the desperate fury of the Castilians who, after killing the Aztec commander, took his banner and hoisted it victoriously.

The Mexicas, full of consternation on discovering that their lord was dead, broke off the offensive and withdrew, disordered and confused. The road to Tlaxcala was open.

THE RECEPTION IN TLAXCALA

The Tlaxcaltecs showed the Spaniards that they were their good friends in the good times as well as the bad. With them they could finally rest and regain strength, even Cortés spent a few days in bed because of illness. The colony of Villa Rica de Veracruz continued to be in Spanish hands and this, although it relaxed the commander, exasperated his sub-

OTUMBA

The Battle of Otumba was the last attempt by the Mexicas to defeat the Spaniards in open battle.

BUILDING THE BRIGANTINES
The Spaniards, with help from their native allies, built the brigantines in Tlaxcala and then transported them on their shoulders to Lake Texcoco.

▼

ordinates. They opined that they could escape from this terrible land by sea and then return with reinforcements. Cortés, however, did not even consider this course of action. Returning to Villacruz meant losing everything. His legal standing continued to be questioned. He had received no news from the Castilian Court about what it thought of his venture. He could only return victorious or succumb.

In one of his official letters to the Emperor Charles, he wrote: *'I remembered that fortune always helps the bold, and that we were Christian and that the Kindness and Mercy of God would not allow us to perish and lose so much noble land.'* So, to put it clearly, he did not even think about retreating to the coast. On the contrary, he was determined to face all the dangers to once again defy the enemy in its capital. His spirit was invincible, and his eloquence overwhelming, because he managed to convince his demoralised army to once again join him in his rash endeavour.

The Aztecs sent an ambassador to the Tlaxcaltecs asking that they join them against the invaders. Fortunately for Cortés, the Council of Tlaxcala instead decided to continue being faithful to the Spaniards. This was much to Cortés' joy, nothing was more agreeable for him than the separation of the natives. The first priority was to restore the prestige of white *teules* in the valley of the Anahuac. In addition, there was nothing better to revive the spirits of the troops than a military expedition.

THE SUBMISSION OF THE VALLEY

The immediate goal was the Tepeacans, a powerful tribe and ally of the Mexicas and, therefore, an enemy of Tlaxcala. Still without artillery and firearms, the battle-hardened soldiers encountered few problems overpowering the city of Tepeaca, where Cortés decided to install his new headquarters. From here forwards, he continued with his policy of overpowering the feudatary cities of Tenochtitlan militarily, while collaborating

Map of the lake where Tenochtitlan lay with the surrounding towns.

◀

with any chief who wanted to free himself from Tenochca control. The Spanish detachments, commanded by Cortés and captains like Alvarado or Sandoval, responded diligently to requests for aid from the tribes of the region.

The Aztec yoke must have been oppressive and cruel because the chieftains willingly formed an alliance with the Spaniards in order to take revenge for the offences inflicted on them by the proud Mexicas. If they had been aware of the destiny that awaited them, they would not have collaborated so gladly with the conquistador's plans. But they were blinded by hatred and superstition.

Conditions markedly improved with the arrival of reinforcements. The Cuban governor knew nothing about Lieutenant Narváez's defeat and sent provisions and men to Mexico under the false assumption that he was providing for his people. Also, further reinforcements arrived from the island of Hispaniola. All of them were seduced by the promise of conquest and headed inland along the route that was once again open and safe for the Spaniards.

In this way, within a few months, Cortés was able to restore his authority in the valley of Mexico. However, the enemy remained resolute and threatening in his capital. The routine ambassadors of peace and submission that Cortés sent to Tenochtitlan were received with contempt. Total war was, therefore, inevitable. Cortés ordered thirteen brigantines to be built in Tlaxcala with the idea of transporting them in pieces on the backs of the native porters twenty leagues over the mountains, re-assembling them and floating them on Lake Texcoco. The Tlaxcaltecs worked hard under the orders of the master carpenter, Martín López.

CUAUHTEMOC
1494-1525

As the last Mexica sovereign, he fought bravely against the conquistadores. Mexican national pride depicts him as one of its national heroes, while the docile submission of Moctezuma sets him down in their history as a traitor and coward.

The name of Cuauhtémoc, 'Eagle that Descends', seems appropriate for the sovereign who governed the city's decline. He came to power when Tenochtitlan was surrounded, rejecting all of Cortés' peace proposals and only surrendering when it was impossible to resist any longer, as the city was almost totally destroyed and his people were dying of hunger and disease.

After being made captive, he was subjected to a cruel torture by the Spaniards at the request of the Royal Treasurer, Julian de Alderete, who was not satisfied with the amount of gold that had been found and wanted more. Cuauhtémoc stoically endured having his feet burnt in the fire, refusing to give information about the whereabouts of any further treasure. Years later he was accused of conspiracy and Cortés ordered his execution.

He died on the 28th February 1525, four years after the fall of Tenochtitlan.

A new element now appeared on the already crowded scene. It was as if the Christian God blessed the work of His people. The plague extended like an apocalyptic rider across the valley, ravaging complete villages. While the Spaniards were immune to its effects, the natives had no defence against this scourge. It was, of course, smallpox, and had been brought by Narváez's men. The virus arrived in the capital resulting in thousands of the inhabitants being struck down, among them the brave *Tlatoani, Cihuacoatl*. The young and hardened Cuauhtémoc, Moctezuma's nephew, was acclaimed as the lord of that suffering city which their Gods had abandoned.

The first movement in the Tenochtitlan campaign was the taking of the city of Texcoco. The refortified Spanish army, accompanied by a considerable Tlaxcaltec contingent, entered the city on the 31st December 1520. They encountered no resistance; its inhabitants, who were following their king to take refuge in Tenochtitlan, had abandoned it.

Cortés took advantage of the now vacant throne to put the Texcocan prince, Ixtlixochitl, on it. Although he was still comparatively young, he was an old and faithful friend of the Spaniards.

Making the city his base camp, the commander organised his campaign to conquer the cities on the shores of Lake Texcoco and isolate Tenochtitlan.

He devastated Iztapalapa and Xochimilco, set up a garrison in Tlacopan and secured control in Chalco by supporting the chieftains against the Mexicas. Cuauhtemoc, on the other hand, had fortified the city and was dedicating his time to hindering, in all ways possible, Cortés work. He even intentionally destroyed the docks to drown the Spaniards when they fought in Iztapalapa but, once again, they miraculously escaped.

When the brigantines eventually arrived from Tlaxcala and were launched on the lake, Cortés was ready to initiate the siege of Tenochtitlan.

BEGINNING OF THE SIEGE

The brigantines were launched with a great display of splendour and fuss, following the policy of the Spaniards of not failing to take advantage of any occasion to dazzle the indigenous people with the European advances.

This was followed by a ceremonial inspection of the troops. Thanks to the latest reinforcements, the Spanish commander now had under his command eighty-seven cavalry, and eight hundred infantrymen, one hundred and eighty of which were harquebusiers and crossbowmen. The artillery consisted of three bombards and fifteen culverins with some falconets, ideal for mounting on the fore or aftcastles of the brigantines. They had ball, powder and fifty thousand copper headed arrows. This was the greatest Spanish army that had been seen in Nueva España and, with the support of the brigantines, Cortés doubtless thought he was in the ideal position to resume his conquest. Three hundred of the men were destined to man the brigantines, half as crew and the rest as soldiers. The Tlaxcaltecs contributed fifty thousand men under the command of the arrogant Xicoténcatl. Strategy for the siege was simple, it was necessary to cut the roads entering the city and then

THE PRISONERS' FATE
Any unfortunate Spaniards who
fell into the hands of the Mexicas
were sacrificed and beheaded. The
Indians displayed the severed
bearded heads to the
conquistadores in a vain attempt
to discourage them.

use the brigantines to extend the blockade on the lake preventing any canoes from passing. Cortés distributed his forces into three divisions. Alvarado was placed in charge at Tlacopan, on the fateful road of the 'Noche Triste', which allowed exit to Tenochtitlan by the west. Cristóbal de Olid, with another third of the forces, took up position on Coyoacan, the city that dominated another section of road that connected with the South road. Both captains received the order to destroy the Chapultepec aqueduct that supplied the city with fresh water.

It was also necessary to complete the destruction of the city of Iztapalapa that had been retaken by the Mexicas. To do this, a joint attack had been planned, by water and by land. The young Gonzalo de Sandoval was in command of the ground troops and Cortés was in charge of the fleet. However, just as the operation was about to commence there was an important desertion from the army. The Tlaxcaltec general Xicoténcatl, who appeared to be the only native conscious of the fact that the Spaniards were perhaps worse enemies than the Aztecs. Incapable of being able to continue taking part in the war, he left the Spanish cause and returned to Tlaxcala, full of resentment.

There was no hesitation on Cortés' part, he ordered the Tlaxcaltec general to be captured and, charging him with desertion before the enemy, executed him. If all the Anahuac chieftains had shared the spirit and vision of Xicoténcatl, the Spaniards could not have conquered Mexico.

OWNERS OF THE LAKE

Cortés considered the fleet of brigantines as *'the key to the war'* and to demonstrate it he needed a good breeze. Sandoval attacked Iztapalapa as ordered. A large fleet of canoes loaded with howling warriors left from nearby Tenochtitlan and advanced quickly towards the Spanish ships. It was the moment to use the brigantines, but there was no wind, the sails hung uselessly from the masts. The canoes were coming dangerously close when, suddenly, a small breeze sprang up. The commander smiled.

On wings of the wind, the brigantines moved majestically over the lake, scattering death and destruction. The cannons and harquebusiers fired with devastating effect into the Indians. The brigantines bows cleaved the canoes, smashing them into pieces and the lake's water soon turned red with the blood of the natives. The victory was total and overwhelming, Cortés was the master of Lake Texcoco.

Cuauhtémoc tried with all his might to resist the superiority of the brigantines, first planting stakes on the lakebed and attracting the brigantines towards the cane plantations where the ships beached on the hidden obstacles. But the stratagem worked only once. From then on, the Castilians sailed with greater caution. Cortés, the master of the lake, decided to switch his headquarters to the fort of Xoloc, an Aztec fortification that protected the point where the roads of Iztapalapa and Coyoacan led to Tenochtitlan by the southern route.

Access from the west and south were now controlled and only the north road of Tepejacac was left to block, a mission that the brave Sandoval successfully carried out.

From here on the strategy of harassment began. Each day, the Spaniards organised simultaneous attacks of two or more divisions supported by the artillery fire of the brigantines. Step-by-step they took control of the canals that blocked the roads, which they then filled up and then continued into the city's interior killing left, right and centre. The Aztecs resisted the pressure of the Spaniards and their allies as much as they were able. At night, the Spaniards returned to their quarters and the besieged took the opportunity to breath, reopen the canals and rebuild the barricades, the reason why, the following day, it was necessary to begin all over again. .

THE DESTRUCTION OF TENOCHTITLAN

However, what caused most damage to the resisting warriors was the cessation of any outside assistance. Despite the blockade, the native canoes continued to deceive the guards on the brigantines and supplied the city with provisions. However, as the success of the Spaniards seemed inevitable, the last cities in the valley, old allies of Tenochtitlan, were abandoned and the people paid tribute to the feared foreigners and stopped sending provisions to Cuauhtémoc and his people.

In spite of the hunger and the onset of plague among the Mexicas, their morale remained high and they continued to show a determined resistance to their enemies. The siege was prolonged, conditions for the

CUAUHTEMOC IS CAPTURED
Cuauhtemoc resisted the Spanish siege until it was manifestly impossible to hold out any longer. He was captured on the lake by a brigantine while trying to escape.

besiegers were not very comfortable either, torrential rains soaked them and they could not rest for a moment. Each morning they attacked, and at night they had to maintain an alert guard to repel the counterattacks of the desperate Mexicas.

The confidence of the native allies began to weaken. As a result of a raid on the main square, where the Spaniards suffered a setback and even the commander was on the verge of falling into the hands of Cuauhtémoc, the priests of Huitzilipochtli proclaimed that its deity had given a period of eight days, after which the Spaniards would be exterminated.

The resolute and credulous spirit of the Anahuac natives caused all the native allies, who did not doubt veracity of the prophecy, to desert the Spaniards.

Cortés and his men maintained their positions during the eight days after which it became obvious that the white God was much more powerful. The allies returned to the fold. Cuauhtémoc continued rejecting the peace proposals. So Cortés issued the order to begin a total war of destruction. '*I decided to take a measure for our safety and to close in on the enemy, and it was as we took ground by the city streets, we destroyed all the houses on one side and the other, so we did not advance without leaving everything desolate, and what was water, we made mainland, however long it took us*', he wrote to the emperor.

This greatest unimaginable desolation broke down the resistance. They died in their thousands from hunger and disease and nobody was strong enough to remove the bodies. The city became an ossuary that quickly decomposed and rotted. On the 13th August 1521, the Spaniards launched their final assault. Although it seemed impossible, the Mexicas still continued to fiercely defend themselves, while many of them tried to flee in canoes across the lake. The emperor Cuauhtémoc was intercepted by a brigantine and taken prisoner before Cortés. As expected, once the Mexicas discovered that *Tlatoani* had been captured, all resistance ended. In a final act of pride, and sincerely wishing not to survive the destruction of his city, Cuauhtémoc pleaded with Cortés to take his life.

However, the commander pardoned him and issued an order stating that the *Tlatoani* and his family were to be treated with the utmost respect. However, greed for gold pushed the Spaniards into vilely torturing the valiant monarch.

The survivors were authorized to leave what was left of the city. Shortly after, the clearing up and reconstruction work began.

The siege had lasted three months, the conquest was complete but Cortés continued to be restless. He had still received no news from Castile either condemning or approving his epic adventure.

◀ THE DESTRUCTION OF THE CITY
To retake Tenochtitlan, the Spaniards had to demolish the city house-by-house and reduce the inhabitants to a dreadful existence.

J. Redondo

AFTER THE CONQUEST

In order to understand the strange silence of the Castilian Court in respect to the conquest of Mexico, it is necessary to consider the situation of Castile at that time. As previously stated, the new sovereign, young Charles, was absent from Spain and absorbed by the European problems of his imperial crown. Castile, meanwhile, was involved in the War of the Communities and the reins of the kingdom were in the hands of Cardinal Adriano de Utrech, Charles' private tutor, who was unlikely to be able to understand the mysterious Spanish character.

In addition to this, the conquistador's sworn enemy, governor Velázquez, had a first rate ally in the Court, Bishop Fonseca, director of the Council of the Indies. From this elevated position, he used his authority to undermine Cortés in any way possible.

This scheming bishop had no problem in convincing the hesitant Adriano to sign an order allowing him to designate a commissioner with absolute power to go to Nueva España (New Spain). The commissioner's mission was to investigate the conduct of the conquistador, suspend him of his functions and even hold him under arrest until such time that the Court had made a definitive decision.

The civil servant empowered by the bishop was one Cristóbal de Tapia and, on his arrival at Villa Rica de Veracruz, he saw that nothing could stand up to such a powerful man as Cortés at that moment. While he had no chance to interview him, he did accept the gold that was generously offered. He returned to Cuba full of hate and maliciousness, adding to the already existing accusations against the conquistador.

Cortés, however, was not without his supporters in Castile. His father, Martín Cortés, worked tirelessly in the interests of his son, ably supported by the Duke of Béjar, a great Spanish noble and a very influential person at the Court.

The Duke's influence convinced the confused Adriano of the great damage that Bishop Fonseca's plot caused to Castile's interests. Finally, the unworthy prelate was dismissed his position.

On the Emperor's return to Spain, it became essential to solve the thorny subject surrounding the legality of the conqueror of Mexico. To decide this, a Meeting that included members of the monarch's Privy Council and the Council of the Indies was convened, who listened patiently to the allegations from both sides.

Velázquez's accusations could do little against the clear achievements of the conquistador and the proven evidence that he had financed two thirds of the expedition himself. The defence asked the Junta (Board) if they were willing to dishonour a man who had faced all obstacles and, using his own resources, had gained for Castile an empire that no other European country possessed.

Cortés' actions were backed without reservation and he was granted the appointment of Governor, Commander in Chief and Greater Justice

MONUMENT TO CORTÉS

A statue of Cortés in his home town of Medellín.

of the Nueva España. His officers were also compensated with honours and wealth and the troops received privileges and concessions of land.

Governor Velázquez no longer held jurisdiction over Nueva España. He was foiled completely in his aspirations for revenge. So, ruined and dishonoured, he fell into a deep melancholy that, a few months later, resulted in his death.

THE DEATH OF CORTÉS

The supreme command bestowed on Cortés, and the timely recognition of his achievements calmed him and his men. It also allowed him moments of peace to embark upon new dreams of exploration and conquest. However, his restless spirit allowed him little rest.

His first task was to lay the foundations of what would become modern Mexico, a racially mixed nation uprooted from its indigenous past. The capital was rebuilt on the same spot and plants, seeds and cattle were imported from Europe. Little-by-little the country's profile changed. As was to be expected, he put much enthusiasm and dedication into evangelism. In this respect, the words of friar Bernardino Sahagún are sadly enlightening:

'We welcomed the chieftains' children into our schools where we taught them how to read, write, and sing. The children of the poor natives gathered in the courtyards and were taught the Christian faith. After teaching, one or two brothers took the pupils to a nearby teocalli where, after a couple of days work it was totally demolished. In this way, they destroyed in just a short time all the Aztec temples, large and small, in such a way that there would be no trace of them.'

The new Commander in Chief did not know how or did not want to peacefully enjoy his conquest. He embarked on numerous expeditions and explorations that ended with him getting into debt, an ignominy that hung over him until the end of his days.

On the other hand, envy, which is very prevalent in the Spanish nature, also allowed him no rest. Unfair accusations were laid against him, such as him wanting to become independent from the crown. These accusations grew ever more intense and he was forced to return to Spain to defend his rights. Emperor Charles once again recognized his merits and bestowed on him the title of Marques of the Valley of Oaxaca and awarded him with immense territories. However, he did agree to hand over the reins of government of his conquest and these ended up in the hands of the Viceroy, Antonio de Mendoza.

This was a common policy of the Spanish Crown, men to conquer a territory and others to govern it. Hernán Cortés passed away on the 2nd of December 1547 at the age of sixty-three, in Castilleja de la Cuesta, Seville. He had returned to Spain for a second time to continue the defence of his interests that he regarded as damaged by the Crown. Exhausted and disillusioned, he was on the way to Mexico once more accompanied by his son, when he died.

CAUSES OF THE CONQUEST

The story of the conquest of an empire by a handful of adventurers is an amazing one. So incredible, that the facts narrated here could scarcely be accepted in a story of fiction.

▲

THE FIRST VICEROY

Antonio Mendoza, first Viceroy of Mexico.

PAST & PRESENT

The cathedral of Mexico City was build over the ruins of the great teocalli of Tenochtitlan.

▼

However, logical causes exist that can explain the rapid collapse of Moctezuma's kingdom and the expansion of the conquest of America in general.

A main and decisive factor in the conquest was the lack of unity that existed between the indigenous tribes. Cortés had an innate ability to use these blind quarrels between the natives to his own benefit. Without the military and logistical support of Tenochtitlan's enemies, the conquest could have lasted centuries instead of just a few years.

On a military level, without doubt the technological superiority of the Europeans gave them remarkable advantages. Not only on the battlefield but also psychologically. The ships, the thunderous cannon and the horses contributed to reinforce the superstitious idea that the invaders were Gods. These ideas were further endorsed by the omens that had announced the arrival of the heirs of Quetzalcoatl at the same time that Cortés disembarked in Veracruz.

The concept of war was also very different in both cultures. In spite of both being belligerent societies, the Mexicans primarily fought to capture their enemies alive and gain power over neighbouring cities in exchange for a tribute. They were unable to conceive the type of war that resulted in total extermination of the opposing side as waged by the Spaniards and even less so the destruction of its religion and culture.

In addition, the Mexica social structure revolved around the religious dependency of the figure of the sovereign. This meant that as soon as the head fell, all the social flock was disoriented.

Another factor of vital importance was the diseases imported from Europe. Recent investigations reveal that the extent of the epidemics was truly apocalyptic in the New World. Smallpox was an important strategic ally in the conquest of Tenochtitlan. The defenceless Mexicas died in their thousands during the siege of the city, debilitating the resistance.

The fatalistic and inexorable sense of existence, imbued in the Mexican spirit by its religion, made them very vulnerable against an adversary with only one true god-almighty, invincible in principle.

BIBLIOGRAPHY

La Filosofía Nahuatl.
Miguel León-Portilla. México 1979

Cómputo Azteca.
David Esparza Hidalgo. México 1975.

México Antiguo.
María Longhena. Editorial Óptima. Barcelona 2001

Las Raíces de América.
J.M. Gómez Tabanera. Madrid 1968.

Vida Cotidiana de los aztecas.
Jacques Soustelle.

Los aztecas.
Victor W. Von Hagen. Editorial Diana. México. 1961

Historia de la Nación Chichimeca.
Fernando Alva de Ixtlixochitl. Historia 16. Madrid 1985

Los Indios de México y Nueva España.
Fray Bartolomé de Las Casas. Editorial Porrúa. México 1974

Historia de los Indios de la Nueva España.
Fray Toribio de Benavente "Motolinía". Alianza Editorial. Madrid 1988

Moctezuma. Germán Vázquez.
Historia 16. Madrid 1987

Historia General de las Cosas de la Nueva España.
Fray Bernardino Sahagún. Editorial Porrúa. México 1975

Cartas de Relación de la Conquista de Méjico.
Hernán Cortés. Espasa-Calpe. Madrid 1970

La Conquista de Méjico.
Francisco López de Gomara. Dastin. Madrid 2001

Fray Bartolomé de las Casas.
Manuel M. Martínez. Madrid 1955

Transculturación y Misión en Nueva España.
Ana de Zaballa. Pamplona 1990

Hernán Cortés y la Mar del Sur.
Miguel León Portilla. Algaba Ediciones. Madrid 2005

Hernán Cortés.
Salvador de Madariaga. Editorial Sudamericana. Buenos Aires 1941

Historia Verdadera de la Conquista de la Nueva España.
Bernal Díaz del Castillo. Ediciones Atlas. Madrid 1947